SKETCHING
ANIMALS

A SKETCHING ANIMALS

Written & Illustrated by Belinda Willson
Additional Illustrations by Greg C Grace
Design & Layout by Jason Willson
Cover Design by Anna Dimasi

FOREWORD

Before commencing any drawing, it is recommended you have at least three different soft pencils, an eraser and a sharpener. 2B, 4B and 6B pencils are preferred and can be purchased from most Art Suppliers and Newsagents.

This book has been designed to encourage the development of good drawing and improve the artist's perception. The studies begin at a relatively easy standard, using a basic four step process to systematically explain the method. The steps are gradually reduced as it is expected the artist will be more aware and techniques, better retained.

As the book progresses, you are encouraged to adopt a more independent approach, thus further enhancing these newly acquired skills.
A series of hints and instructions are included for each illustration.

Good Luck on your path to better drawing!

ISBN: 1 86476 436 8

Axiom
Australia
www.axiompublishing.com.au

Printed in Malaysia

PHYSICAL CHARACTERISTICS

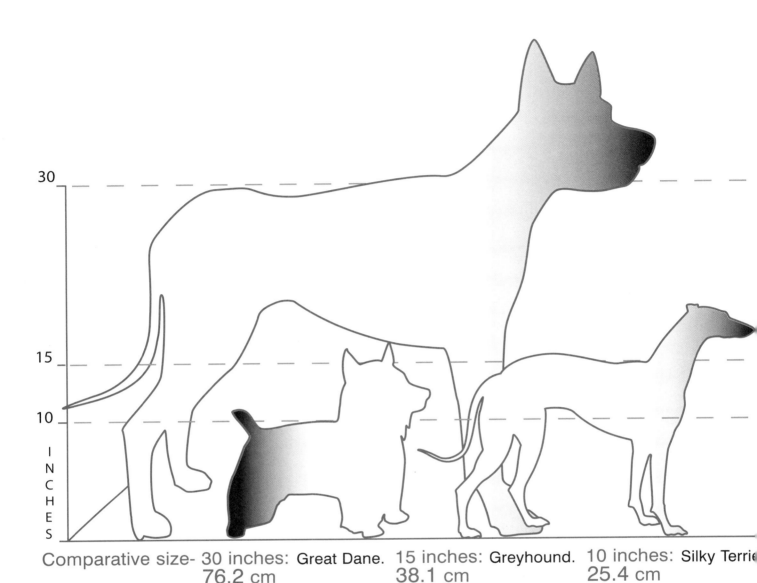

Comparative size- 30 inches: Great Dane. 15 inches: Greyhound. 10 inches: Silky Terrie
76.2 cm   38.1 cm   25.4 cm

OBSERVATION DETAILS:

Dogs come in many different shapes and sizes determined by the structure of the head, body and legs. Of course, colour and length of hair type play their parts in adding to that variation, but just for the moment let us look at the actual structure of the dog. Firstly the head, revealing two basic shapes, a narrow head with a long snout and a wide head with a short snout. Ears may be long or short, erect or down. The neck is significant depending on the breed. The body of all dogs contains 27 bones from the skull to the start of the tail. The legs and paws are used for standing, moving, scratching, and in some breeds, digging. All these structural differences are seen in the wide variety shown within this book. This stated, we should always recognise the variations between breeds, mostly created through human intervention with practical usage being the main intention, i.e. working dogs such as border collies and spaniels, toy dogs such as the chihuahua, fighting dogs such as the bull terrier, and guard dogs in the case of the doberman.

SKELETAL

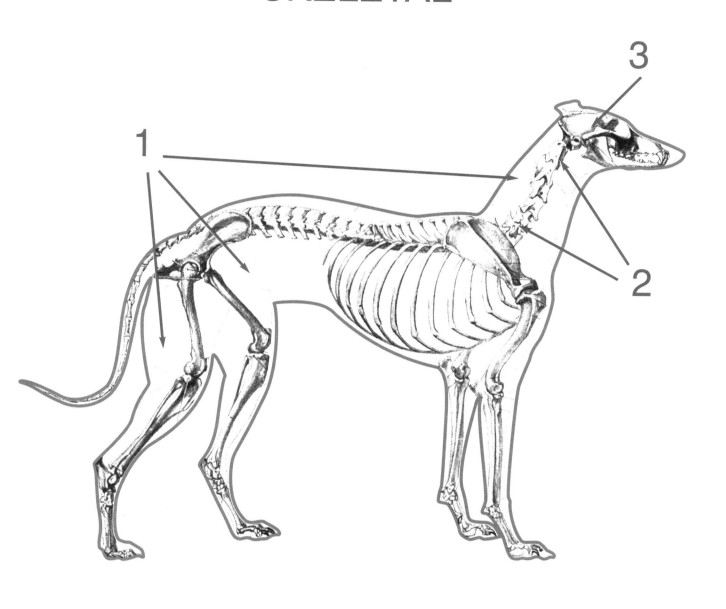

OBSERVATION DETAILS:

The skeletal frame of the dog is strong providing very good protection to vital organs and excellent anchors for its complex muscle system.

1. Notice the bare areas inside the body framework, taken up largely by muscle tissue, supporting and strengthening the skeleton of the dog.

2. The neck bones of the dog are strong and flexible. They have an inter-connective quality helping to provide the agility needed by the dog in its wide range of head and neck movements.

3. The head of the dog is largely bone mass, and almost the entire shape of the head is determined by the skeletal frame within.

PHYSICAL CHARACTERISTICS

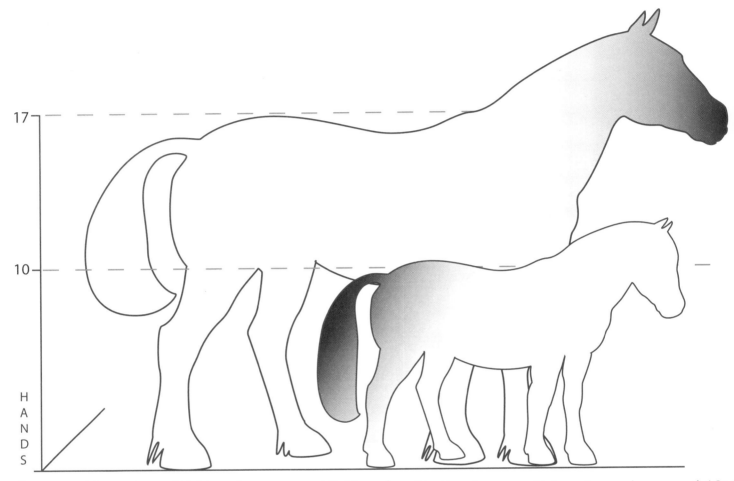

17

10

H
A
N
D
S

Comparitive size- 17 Hands: Shire. 10 Hands: Shetland pony. (1 hand equals around 10c

Horses display a wide variation in size, general body shape and colour of coat. Horses are measured from the ground to the elevated part of the spine, called the withers, between the neck and the back. The measurement is made in hands, with one hand equal to about 10cm o 4 inches. Generally a fully grown horse stands between 14 and 16 hands, although the tallest was measured at a full 18 hands.

Horses have the largest eyes of any land mammal, which protrude from the sides of the head, giving it an extremely wide field of vision. Long legs making the horse a very efficient runner, giving it speed, strength and endurance.

SKELETAL

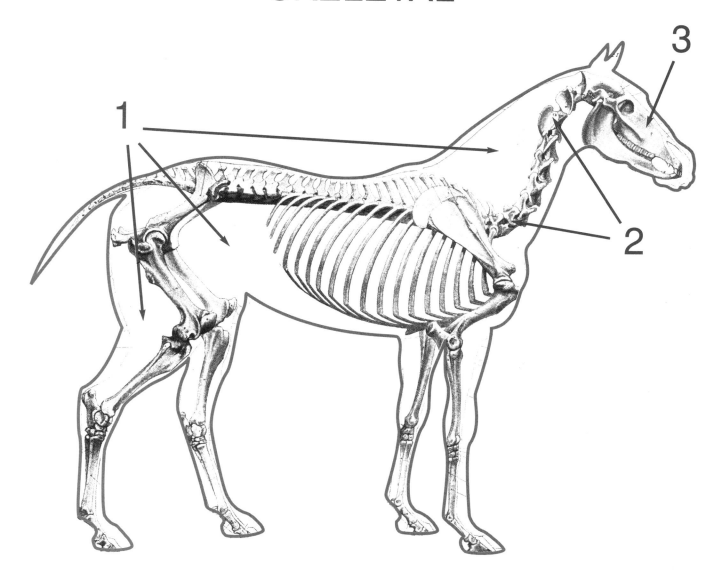

OBSERVATION DETAILS:

The skeletal frame of the horse is understandably strong and supportive. The back leg bones are the largest and most dense in nature as these provide most of the horse's strength when galloping.

1. Notice the bare areas inside the body framework which are largely taken up by muscle tissue supporting and strengthening the skeletal mass.

2. The neck bones of the horse are huge when compared with other animals. They have a unique 'S' shape curve which helps provide the agility needed in the wide range of head and neck movements.

3. The head is largely bone mass, and almost the entire shape is determined by the skeletal frame supporting it.

PHYSICAL CHARACTERISTICS

Comparative size- 126 Inches: Elephant. 63 Inches: Horse. 28 Inches: Lion. (at shoulders)
230 cm   160 cm   71 cm

OBSERVATION DETAILS:

Drawing animals from life is substantially different from drawing humans. Firstly, the illustrator can ask a human to pose, however animals tend to move about making it necessary to initially make fast, and rough sketches. Once this rough is done, fine-tuning can start, adding details as you proceed. Making quick sketches this way assists in heightening your observation skills ensuring more accurate illustration. Obvious things to observe when sketching any animal are size, shape, colour, number of legs, horns, how the animal moves and its outer covering. Once all these details are captured the initial sketch you may then leisurely observe and add muscle tone, skin or fur texture, claw size, shape and any facial expressions.

If life drawing is not for you, there is always illustrating from photographs. This, of course, freezes the action and eliminates the need for hastily drawn roughs, however it may also limit your ability to make fine and accurate observation. Until becoming comfortable sketching from life, this is the next best alternative.

SKELETAL

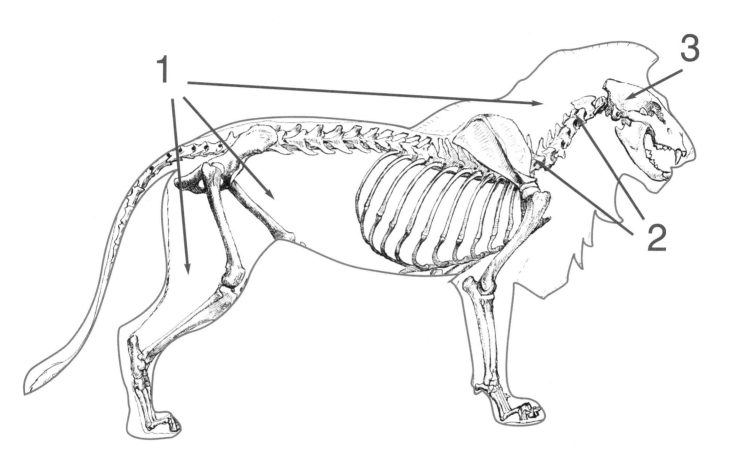

OBSERVATION DETAILS:

1. Notice the bare areas within the body framework. These are largely consumed by muscle tissue supporting and strengthening the skeletal mass.

2. The neck bones of the lion are strong and flexible. They have a unique connection system helping to provide agility needed by the lion in its wide range of head and neck movements.

3. The head is largely bone mass, and almost the entire shape of the head is determined and supported by the skeletal frame.

ANATOMY

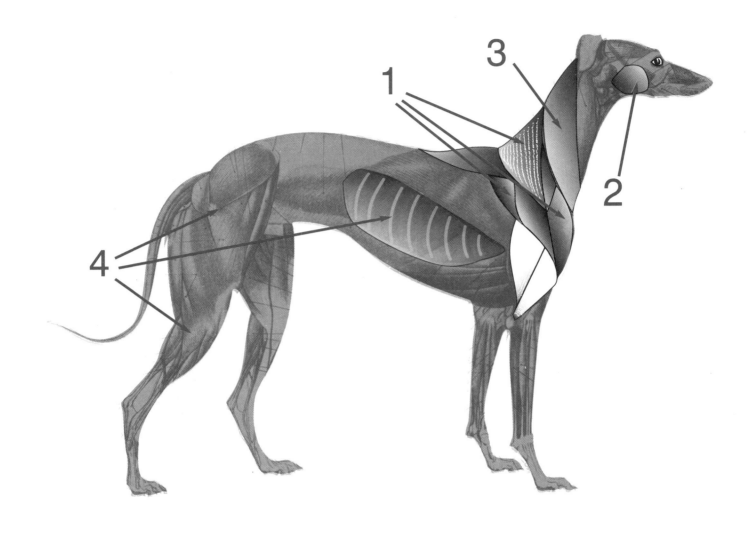

OBSERVATION DETAILS:

By having a broad awareness of the main muscular system the illustrator can more fully understand the movement of dogs. When a muscle contracts or relaxes it pulls on the bone to which it is attached creating movement. Every muscle is paired with another which exerts an opposite force allowing the dog to engage in a wide variety of complex movements. The muscles of the dog are very strong giving power and speed.

1. Notice the complex muscle structure around the shoulders and neck areas.

2. The jaw muscles are rather large and pronounced.

3. The size of the muscular planes are an indication of the strength needed in that area of the anatomy to support the surrounding structure of the body.

4. The dog has chiselled body lines, a robust frame and a firm foothold. The rib cage is long and contoured to support the large stomach and intestines of the dogs' digestive system.

PROFILE

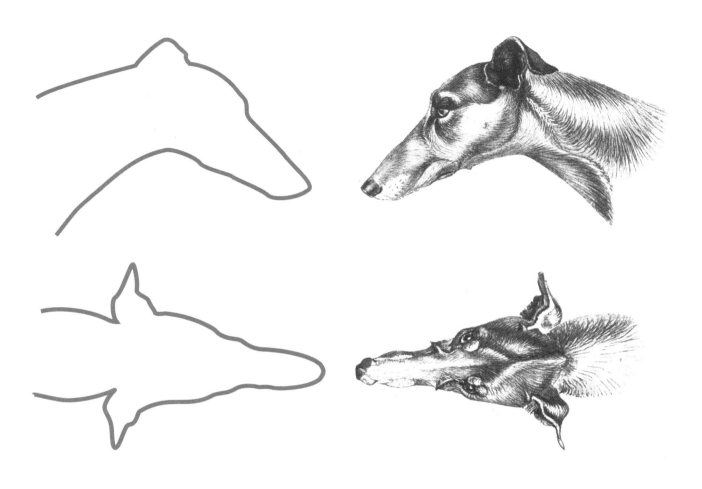

OBSERVATION DETAILS:

These two profiles show the outline form which is the first stage for this style of drawing. Once the angle of the profile is set, the detailing of the shadows and highlights can be included. In this case there are no extreme angles to the profile other than a direct side-on and direct downward view. For this reason the main details giving a pronounced effect to the profile are the darkest shadow areas. A great way to start is with the main dark areas, progressing along to the finer shadow areas and lines. Remember to leave some clear white areas as these make the shadows appear deeper and more defined.

ANATOMY

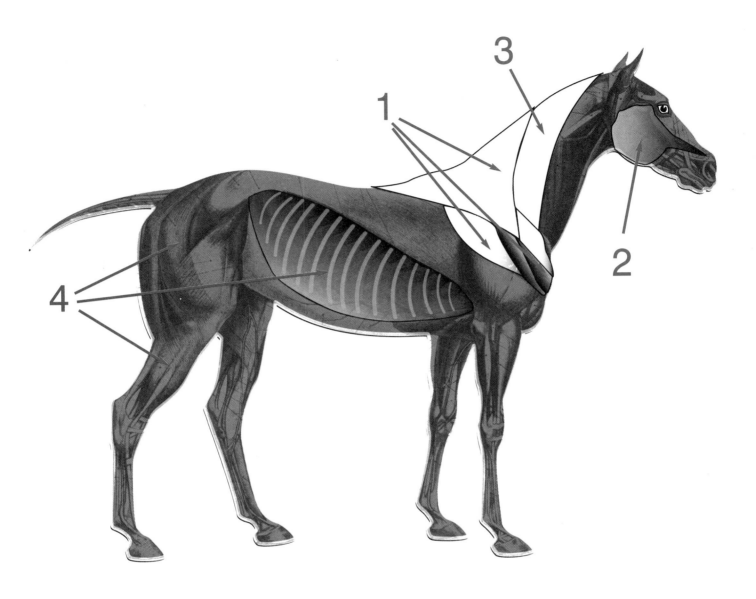

OBSERVATION DETAILS:

The horse has a great deal of muscular development. Considering these areas is most helpful when drawing the horse in detail, and especially in different postures.

1. Notice the complex muscle structure around the shoulders and neck areas.

2. The jaw muscles which are rather large and pronounced.

3. The size of the muscular planes are an indication of the strength needed in that area of the anatomy to support the surrounding structure of the body.

4. The horse has chiselled body lines, a robust frame and a firm foothold. The ribcage is long and contoured, supporting the large stomach and intestines of the digestive system.

PROFILE

OBSERVATION DETAILS:

This very simple profile of the horse's head is static, allowing us to firstly focus on the base outline and then the continuing detail.

1. Side-on profiles as in the one on the opposite page are an ideal way to familiarise with basic shapes and lines, showing the horse's form, both physical and structural.

2. Knowing the basic structure and perspective of the horse as detailed on the previous pages will be helpful before beginning a profile drawing, ensuring correct proportion and overall symmetry.

3. A useful tip, particularly with profiles, is to see the horse as you would a photograph, indicative of an actual pose for the image.

ANATOMY DRAWING

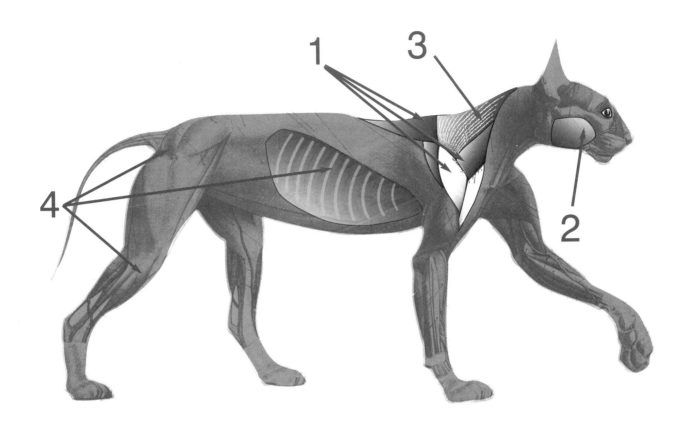

OBSERVATION DETAILS:

This anatomical drawing is from the species of large carnivorous cats including the lion, tiger, and panther.

1. Notice the complex muscle structure within the shoulders and neck areas.

2. As well, the jaw muscles of the cat are rather large and pronounced.

3. The size of the muscular planes are an indication of the strength needed in that area of the anatomy to support the surrounding structure of the body.

4. The cat has sleek body lines with an agile frame and a firm foothold. The ribcage is long and contoured.

PROFILE DRAWING

OBSERVATION DETAILS:

These profiles show in outline form the main step of profile drawing. Once the angle of the profile is set, the detailing of shadows and highlights can be concluded. Obviously there are no angles to this profile, rather a directly side-on view. This being the case the emphasis on the main features will appear as darker shadings. It is therefore suggested that these darker features form the starting point for further shadowed areas. Start here with the main dark areas, progressing to the finer shadow areas and lines. Leaving some clear white areas because they reveal shadows as both deeper and more defined.

PUG

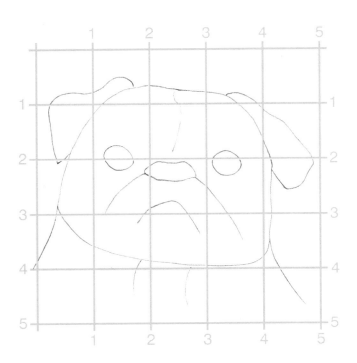

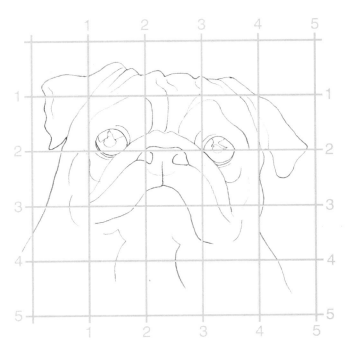

STEP 1:
On your own piece of paper, begin by very lightly drawing a twenty-five square grid using a ruler. A standard 2B pencil is ideal to draw basic circles and lines, as well as the main shapes of the finished sketch. Use the grid to help create accurate proportions.

STEP 2:
Lightly sketching, follow the basic shapes you have just created and develop the outline of the image and its features. Still focusing on proportions and accuracy.

STEP 3:
When satisfied with your outlines, use an eraser to tidy any unnecessary lines or mistakes.

STEP 4:
Using a 4B and a 6B pencil to lightly render the image, copy the techniques shown in the example and read the observation details to help achieve an accurate result.

Sketching Animals

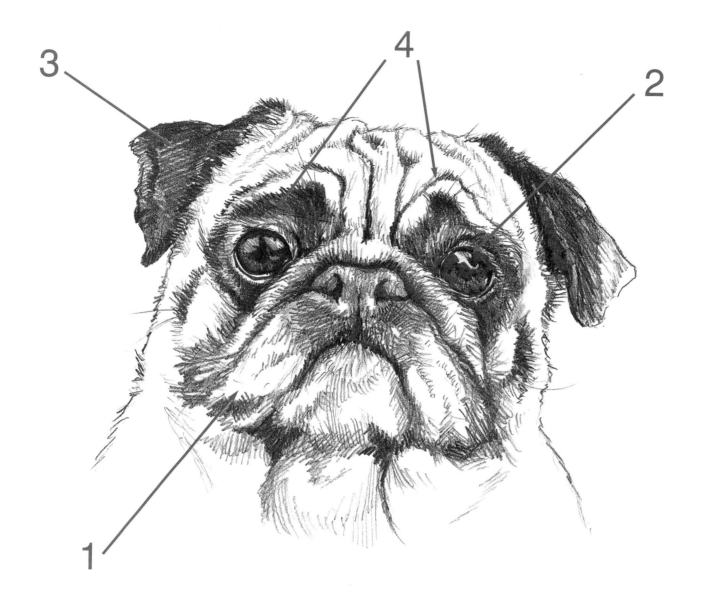

3

4

2

1

OBSERVATION DETAILS:

1. To draw more attention to the facial features and create greater highlights on the Pug's fur, allow the white paper to come through within the drawing. This provides contrast to the darker areas.

2. When drawing the eyes, it is important to keep the illusion of wetness and shine. Shade carefully around the reflections. When the rest of the eye is completed, the darker features can be finished with a 2B pencil, only lightly does it.

3. For effectively darker shadows, use your 6B pencil. This is a soft pencil and there's no need to press too firmly, otherwise damage or denting of the paper may occur.

4. Eyes seriously influence facial expression, as eyebrows do on a human face. To achieve effective colouring above the eye, wrinkles should be shown as raised, giving that classic Pug look.

SHETLAND PONY

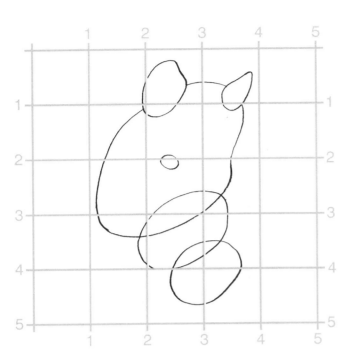

STEP 1:

On your own piece of paper, begin by very lightly drawing a twenty-five square grid using a ruler. A standard 2B pencil is ideal to draw basic circles and lines, as well as the main shapes of the finished sketch. Use the grid to help create accurate proportions.

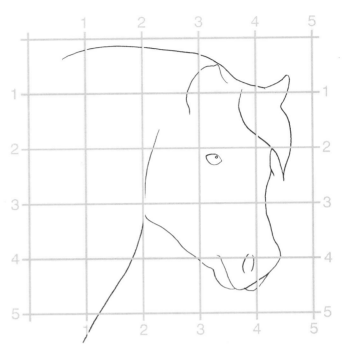

STEP 2:

Lightly sketching, follow the basic shapes you have just created and develop the outline of the image and its features. Still focusing on proportions and accuracy.

STEP 3:

When satisfied with your outlines, use an eraser to tidy any unnecessary lines or mistakes.

STEP 4:

Using a 4B and a 6B pencil to lightly render the image, copy the techniques shown in the example and read the observation details to help achieve an accurate result.

Sketching Animals

OBSERVATION DETAILS:

1. Both facial features and head shape are very important when learning to draw horses and ponies. Concentrate on recreating these aspects with detail and accuracy.

2. Light strokes of the pencil should be used to show the illusion of thick hair, particularly for the pony. Heavy strokes are unwarranted as this will lessen the light, furry effect.

3. The neck can be shown as simple tapered lines, drawing the viewer's attention to the facial features, which of course, is intended in this instance.

AMERICAN TREE FROG

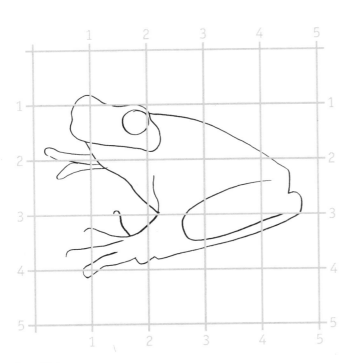

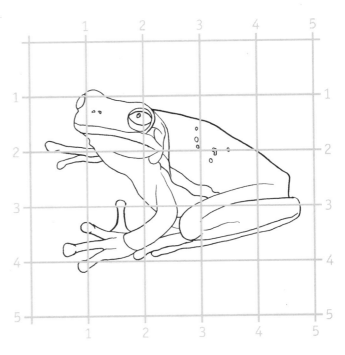

STEP 1:

On your own piece of paper, begin by very lightly drawing a twenty-five square grid using a ruler. A standard 2B pencil is ideal to draw basic circles and lines, as well as the main shapes of the finished sketch. Use the grid to help create accurate proportions.

STEP 2:

Lightly sketching, follow the basic shapes already created and develop the outline of the image and its features. Still focusing on proportions and accuracy.

STEP 3:

When satisfied with your outlines, use an eraser to tidy any unnecessary lines or mistakes.

STEP 4:

Using a 4B and 6B pencil to lightly render the image, copy the techniques shown in the example and read the observation details to help achieve an accurate result.

Sketching Animals

OBSERVATION DETAILS:

1. The stripe along the frog is pale, comparing it with the rest of the body. This area must be rendered in a lighter shade and should be clearly distinguishable.

2. The frog has moisture on its skin, shown by the reflections of light upon its body. In areas of highlight, leave small patches of white to evoke this sense of moisture, contrasting with the texture of the skin.

3. The skin is smooth and should be shaded accordingly. It is recommended you use the side of a 4B pencil, therefore avoiding harsher brush strokes.

MIXED BREED 1

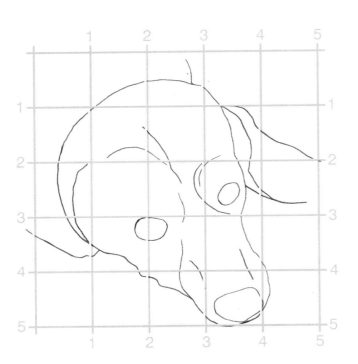

STEP 1:
On your own piece of paper, begin by very lightly drawing a twenty-five square grid using a ruler. A standard 2B pencil is ideal to draw basic circles and lines, as well as the main shapes of the finished sketch. Use the grid to help create accurate proportions.

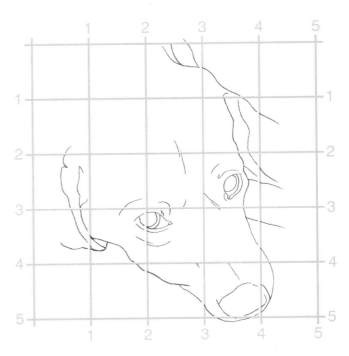

STEP 2:
Lightly sketching, follow the basic shapes you have just created and develop the outline of the image and its features. Still focusing on proportions and accuracy.

STEP 3:
When satisfied with your outlines, use an eraser to tidy any unnecessary lines or mistakes.

STEP 4:
Using a 4B and a 6B pencil to lightly render the image, copy the techniques shown in the example and read the observation details to help achieve an accurate result.

Sketching Animals

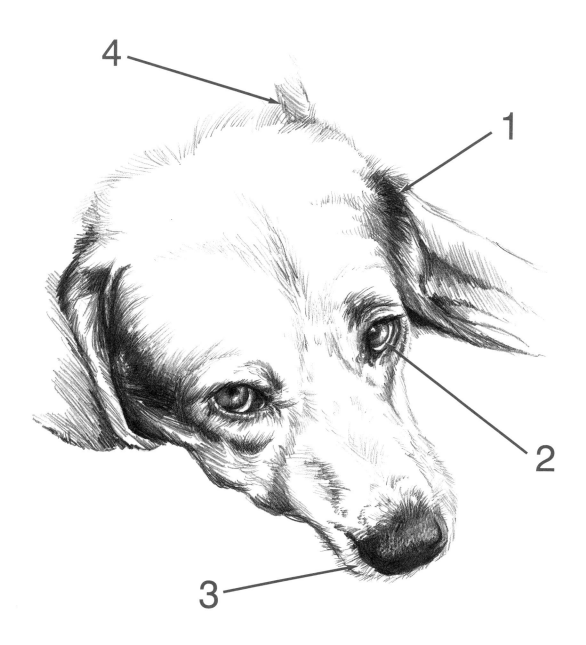

OBSERVATION DETAILS:

1. Focusing on the shadows, gradually build on these by beginning softly, then increasing the density of application as confidence grows. Remembering colouring can always be darkened but lightening lines can be difficult!

2. The main focal point with this portrait is the eyes. Pay particular attention to maintaining their soulful expression, as this helps create the particular mood for the piece.

3. The nasal zone has a different texture to it. This should be subtle, yet noticeable. To achieve this, maintain rendering light enough to appreciate the created patterns.

4. The entire head does not need to be drawn to create an impact. Here the composition draws attention to the eyes and their expression. The edges can be left unfinished to give a mere suggestion as to the dogs laying position.

CONNEMARA

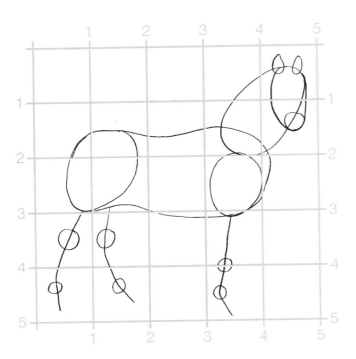

STEP 1:

On your own piece of paper, begin by very lightly drawing a twenty-five square grid using a ruler. A standard 2B pencil is ideal to draw basic circles and lines, as well as the main shapes of the finished sketch. Use the grid to help create accurate proportions.

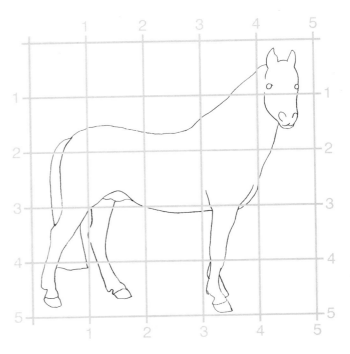

STEP 2:

Lightly sketching, follow the basic shapes you have just created and develop the outline of the image and its features. Still focusing on proportions and accuracy.

STEP 3:

When satisfied with your outlines, use an eraser to tidy any unnecessary lines or mistakes.

STEP 4:

Using a 4B and a 6B pencil to lightly render the image, copy the techniques shown in the example and read the observation details to help achieve an accurate result.

OBSERVATION DETAILS:

1. The Connemara has a small pony-sized head with small, fine ears, intelligent eyes and mobile nostrils. These characteristics should of course be reflected within your sketch.

2. Note also the presence of longer hair on the fetlocks near the hooves. This should be noticeable but not excessively long.

3. Muscles on the legs and hindquarters should be obviously displayed. Begin drawing these features by shading lightly with the side of your 4B or 6B pencil. Gradually increasing rendering without leaving hard edges.

4. Giving the illusion of thicker sections to the mane and tail, apply heavier rendering along the neck with a few particular strands, leaving lighter sections to indicate depth in the hair.

KANGAROO

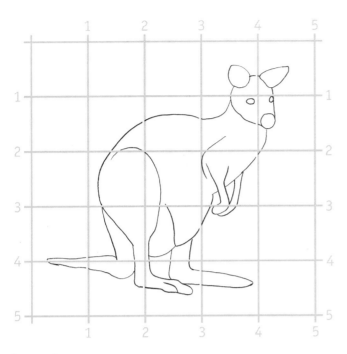

STEP 1:

On your own piece of paper, begin by very lightly drawing a twenty-five square grid using a ruler. A standard 2B pencil is ideal to draw basic circles and lines, as well as the main shapes of the finished sketch. Use the grid to help create accurate proportions.

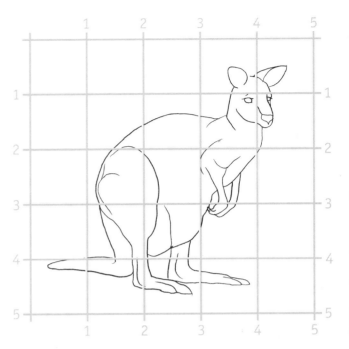

STEP 2:

Lightly sketching, follow the basic shapes already created and develop the outline of the image and its features. Still focusing on proportions and accuracy.

STEP 3:

When satisfied with your outlines, use an eraser to tidy any unnecessary lines or mistakes.

STEP 4:

Using a 4B and 6B pencil to lightly render the image, copy the techniques shown in the example and read the observation details to help achieve an accurate result.

Sketching Animals

OBSERVATION DETAILS:

1. The kangaroo has oversized hind legs and feet when compared to the smaller front arms and paws. Use the length of your pencil to check measurements of these features against your own illustration.

2. The tail is long, very heavy and should be drawn accordingly, noting the tail falls straight down and then trails along the ground.

3. The eye area is quite dark. Although over-rendering this area should be monitored as the eyes and facial features may lose their impact.

4. The eyes are focussed on something in the foreground off to the right, catching the kangaroo's attention. The ears should be turned in the same direction, giving the more alert expression.

MIXED BREED 2

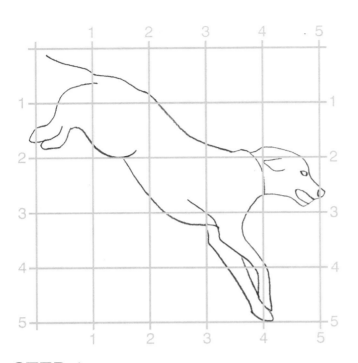

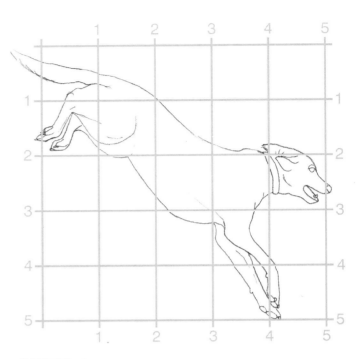

STEP 1:

On your own piece of paper, begin by very lightly drawing a twenty-five square grid using a ruler. A standard 2B pencil is ideal to draw basic circles and lines, as well as the main shapes of the finished sketch. Use the grid to help create accurate proportions.

STEP 2:

Lightly sketching, follow the basic shapes you have just created and develop the outline of the image and its features. Still focusing on proportions and accuracy.

STEP 3:

When satisfied with your outlines, use an eraser to tidy any unnecessary lines or mistakes.

STEP 4:

Using a 4B and a 6B pencil to lightly render the image, copy the techniques shown in the example and read the observation details to help achieve an accurate result.

Sketching Animals

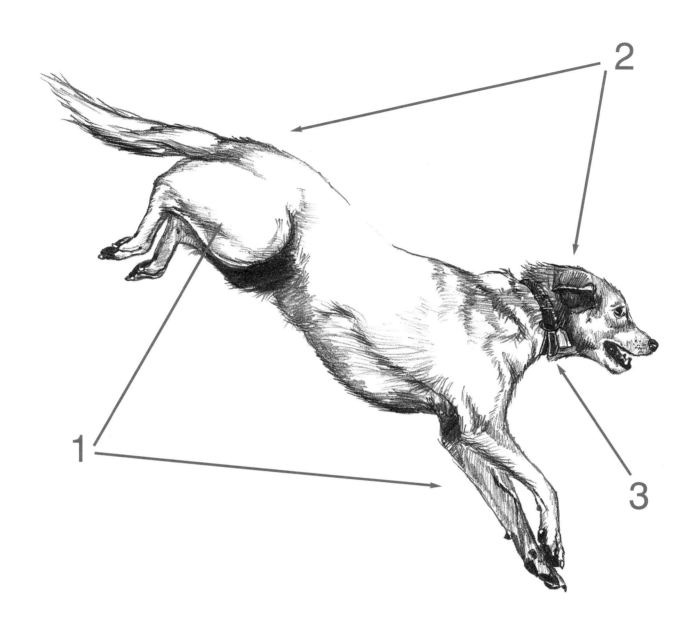

OBSERVATION DETAILS:

1. A dog's body has many powerful muscles, allowing it to effectively run and jump. Notice how the hind legs curl up and the front legs stretch out as it prepares to land. Make sure the angles and positions of the legs are accurately drawn.

2. The position of the dog's head, legs and body mass are at quite an exaggerated angle. This creates the illusion he has jumped over something very large. If this angle is incorrect the dog will seem unbalanced. If uncertain of the correct positioning, use a pencil to make the same angle as the example shown, then keeping that angle, follow it across to your own drawing. This will indicate accuracy and with a few adjustments, this will reveal the greatest proficiency.

3. When drawing a dog portrait, or any portrait for that matter; it is helpful to include personal items such as a dog collar, a favourite toy, or objects significant to that subject. This adds further visual interest to the composition and shows their personality and character.

THOROUGHBRED FOAL

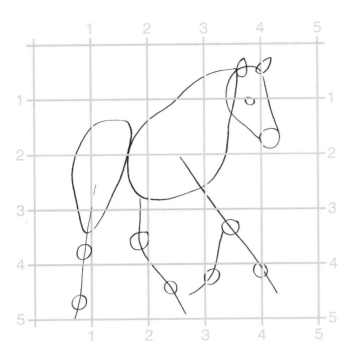

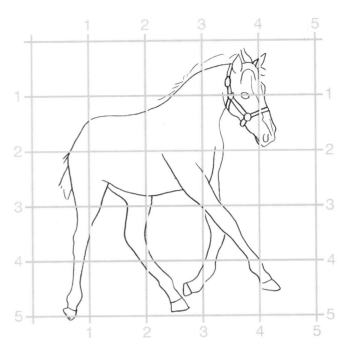

STEP 1:

On your own piece of paper, begin by very lightly drawing a twenty-five square grid using a ruler. A standard 2B pencil is ideal to draw basic circles and lines, as well as the main shapes of the finished sketch. Use the grid to help create accurate proportions.

STEP 2:

Lightly sketching, follow the basic shapes you have just created and develop the outline of the image and its features. Still focusing on proportions and accuracy.

STEP 3:

When satisfied with your outlines, use an eraser to tidy any unnecessary lines or mistakes.

STEP 4:

Using a 4B and a 6B pencil to lightly render the image, copy the techniques shown in the example and read the observation details to help achieve an accurate result.

Sketching Animals

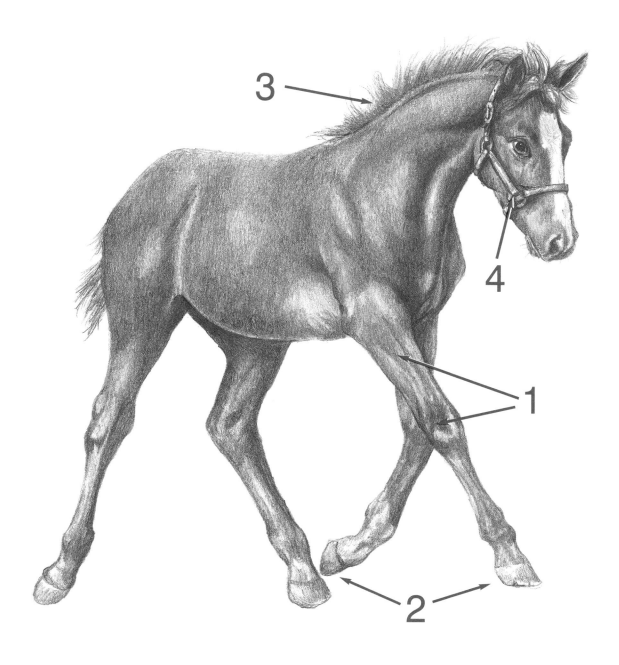

OBSERVATION DETAILS:

1. This foal has long legs, a feature of the breed and its youth. Note where the knee joints are as well as the size and position of tendons and muscles.

2. The angle which hooves are drawn can impact greatly on the realism of a sketch.

   Pay particular attention to their shape and how they are placed on the ground.

3. The foal has a much smaller mane and tail than a full-grown horse. Be careful not to get too enthusiatic by drawing too much hair.

4. By adding the head halter, the composition is enhanced and given a little more detail toward the overall interest of the piece.

ELEPHANT

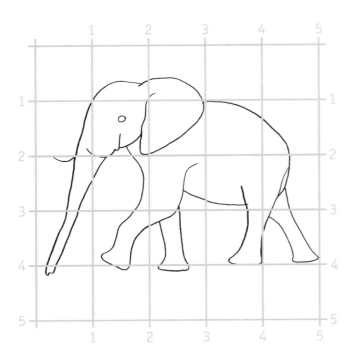

STEP 1:

On your own piece of paper, begin by very lightly drawing a twenty-five square grid using a ruler. A standard 2B pencil is ideal to draw basic circles and lines, as well as the main shapes of the finished sketch. Use the grid to help create accurate proportions.

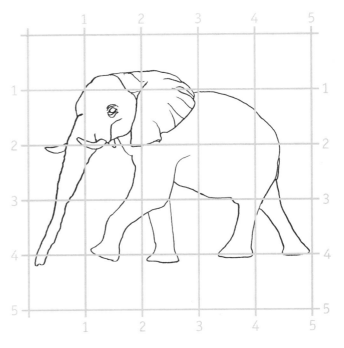

STEP 2:

Lightly sketching, follow the basic shapes already created and develop the outline of the image and its features. Still focusing on proportions and accuracy.

STEP 3:

When satisfied with your outlines, use an eraser to tidy any unnecessary lines or mistakes.

STEP 4:

Using a 4B and 6B pencil to lightly render the image, copy the techniques shown in the example and read the observation details to help achieve an accurate result.

Sketching Animals

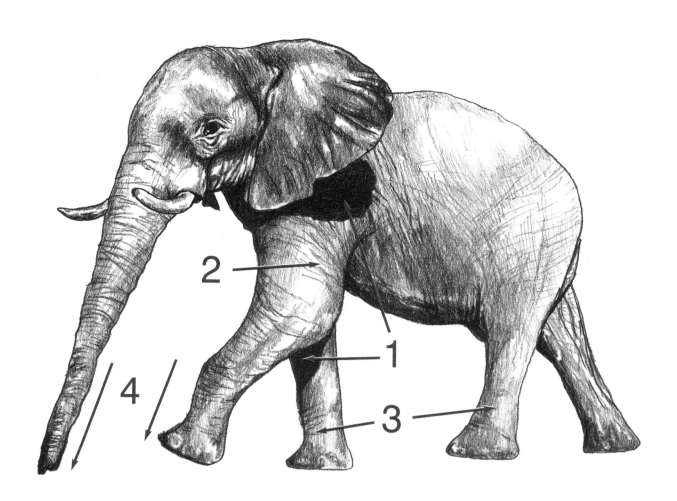

OBSERVATION DETAILS:

1. The darkest parts of this composition are shadows behind the ears and legs. All other sections displaying shadow should be a few tones lighter.

2. The elephant has thick skin with repeated wrinkles upon it. These drawn lightly over the areas of highlight, therefore not dominating the illustration.

3. The elephant's weight is placed on the two legs in the middle of the composition. The other two legs, at the front and rear, should be positioned slightly raised therefore ensuring weight distribution appears in perspective. Also aiding in the expression of movement.

4. The trunk should be drawn at the correct length and parallel to the raised front leg.

GOLDEN RETRIEVER

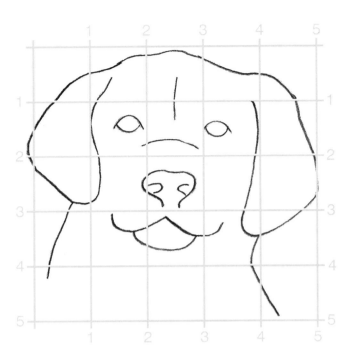

STEP 1:

On your own piece of paper, begin by very lightly drawing a twenty-five square grid using a ruler. A standard 2B pencil is ideal to draw basic circles and lines, as well as the main shapes of the finished sketch. Use the grid to help create accurate proportions.

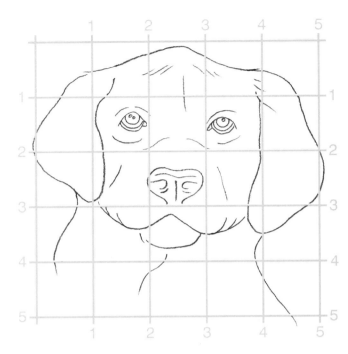

STEP 2:

Lightly sketching, follow the basic shapes you have just created and develop the outline of the image and its features. Still focusing on proportions and accuracy.

STEP 3:

When satisfied with your outlines, use an eraser to tidy any unnecessary lines or mistakes.

STEP 4:

Using a 4B and a 6B pencil to lightly render the image, copy the techniques shown in the example and read the observation details to help achieve an accurate result.

Sketching Animals

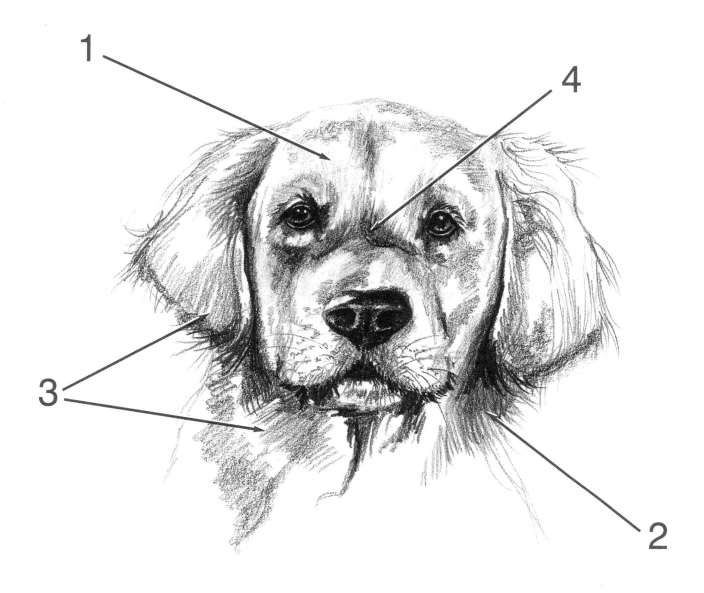

OBSERVATION DETAILS:

1. Start softly, then create density using further strokes. Use this to emphasise specific features. Practise on a separate piece of paper until confident with the application. This will remove the hard edge from shading and make it more consistent.

2. Trying to create realistic long fur on an animal, requires irregular strokes. Otherwise the fur will be seen as too much in the same direction and have less perceived movement.

3. The fur of the Golden Retriever is a light colour, as their name suggests. Be careful when rendering and creating flowing strokes for the hair, ensuring the fur does not appear too dark through excessive strokes.

4. The shadows above the muzzle and eye sockets should be of a medium tone, yet still dark enough to bring the nose forward. This will create a three-dimensional effect, with darker tones under the ears and along the folds of the mouth. Shadows around the nose however should be shaded significantly lighter.

ARABIAN

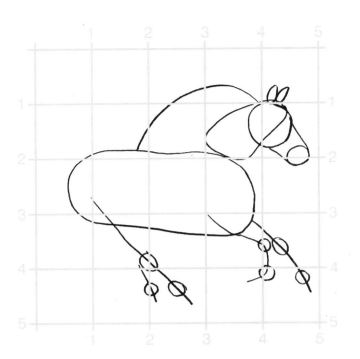

STEP 1:

On your own piece of paper, begin by very lightly drawing a twenty-five square grid using a ruler. A standard 2B pencil is ideal to draw basic circles and lines, as well as the main shapes of the finished sketch. Use the grid to help create accurate proportions.

STEP 2:

Lightly sketching, follow the basic shapes you have just created and develop the outline of the image and its features. Still focusing on proportions and accuracy.

STEP 3:

When satisfied with your outlines, use an eraser to tidy any unnecessary lines or mistakes.

STEP 4:

Using a 4B and a 6B pencil to lightly render the image, copy the techniques shown in the example and read the observation details to help achieve an accurate result.

Sketching Animals

OBSERVATION DETAILS:

1. Whilst galloping, both the mane and tail must be drawn to show movement. Varying the direction in which the strands fall further emphasises the speed and agility. Tapering the hair by flicking the pencil at the end of each stroke successfully accomplishes the appearance of movement.

2. The hindleg on the opposite side should be rendered heavier than the others, as it falls in shadow. A suggestion of grass gives a greater sense of movement and realism.

3. When drawing the body, muscles and tendons on the legs, hindquarters and shoulders must be accurate. Inaccurately shown, the horse will be seen as out of proportion.

4. Showing alertness, the Arabian's ears should be forward and erect. The steadfast gaze of its eyes will also confirm high spirits and forthrightness.

BLACK RHINOCEROS

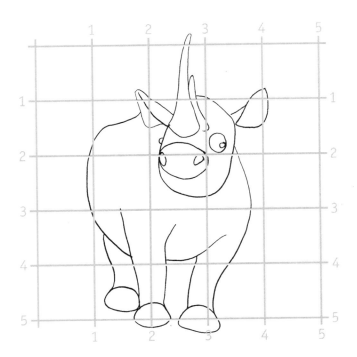

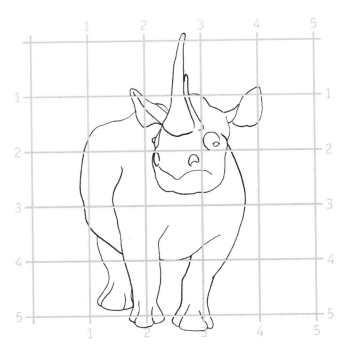

STEP 1:

On your own piece of paper, begin by very lightly drawing a twenty-five square grid using a ruler. A standard 2B pencil is ideal to draw basic circles and lines, as well as the main shapes of the finished sketch. Use the grid to help create accurate proportions.

STEP 2:

Lightly sketching, follow the basic shapes already created and develop the outline of the image and its features. Still focusing on proportions and accuracy.

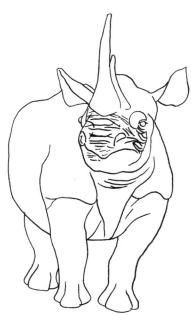

STEP 3:

When satisfied with your outlines, use an eraser to tidy any unnecessary lines or mistakes.

STEP 4:

Using a 4B and 6B pencil to lightly render the image, copy the techniques shown in the example and read the observation details to help achieve an accurate result.

Sketching Animals

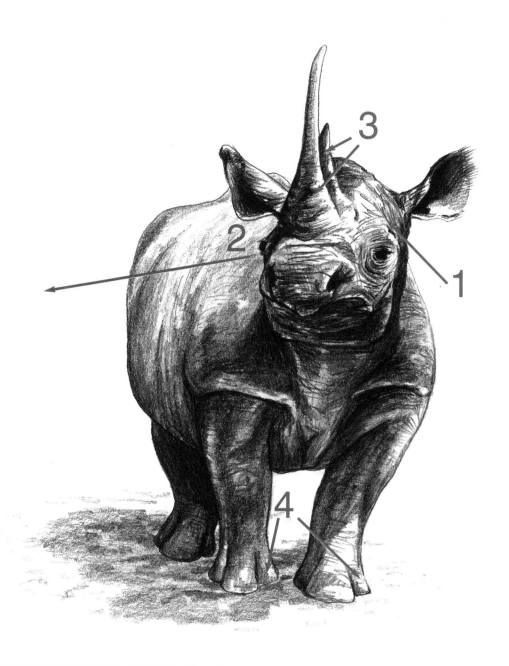

OBSERVATION DETAILS:

1. The rhinoceros is substantially wrinkled on the majority of skin. This effect should be drawn lightly over the top of your rendering, naturally without dominating.

2. The Rhino is looking toward the left of the page. The eyes and head should follow this gaze.

3. The horns on his head and the pointed lip are particular characteristics of the Black Rhinoceros and need to be copied accurately.

4. The Rhino's toes are spread across the ground, creating a firm foundation for supporting the heavy body. The way in which the toes angle outwards indicate the strength of this animal.

AFGHAN

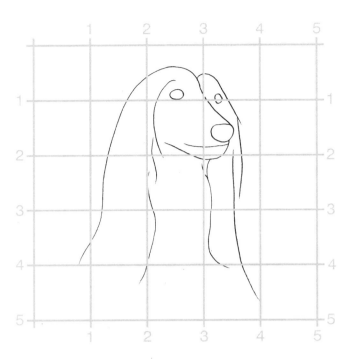

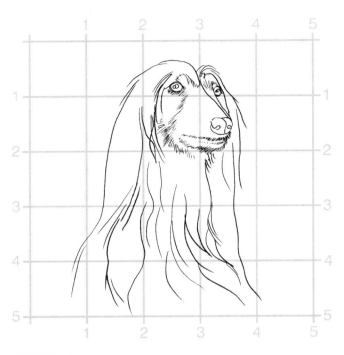

STEP 1:

On your own piece of paper, begin by very lightly drawing a twenty-five square grid using a ruler. A standard 2B pencil is ideal to draw basic circles and lines, as well as the main shapes of the finished sketch. Use the grid to help create accurate proportions.

STEP 2:

When satisfied with this outline stage, erase unnecessary lines or mistakes so your illustration is both neat and well-proportioned.

STEP 3:

Using a 4B and a 6B pencil to lightly render the image, copy the techniques shown in the example and read the observation details, to help achieve an accurate result.

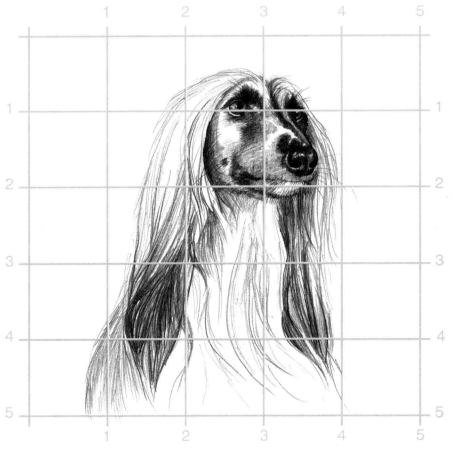

Sketching Animals

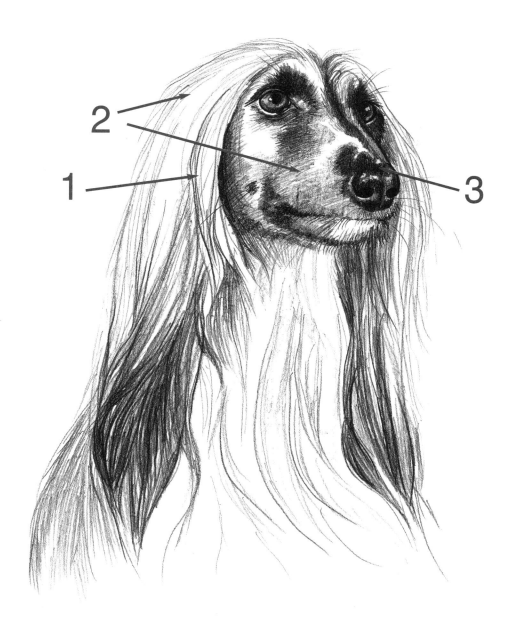

OBSERVATION DETAILS:

1. The Afghan has such long hair, hiding the presence of the accompanying long ears. The darker fur at the base of the ear's hair becomes important, as this is the only defining feature to indicate where the ears end.

2. Rendering fur of different colours when drawing in graphite (black and white) can be a challenge. Each shade must look different to the next. Begin rendering the hair on the top of the head and around the muzzle as one is black and should be the darker. The other is a tan colour, which should appear half as dark. The chest hair, as this is white, requires little rendering.

3. The Afghan's nose or muzzle, is very long, and is characteristic of this breed. In this pose however, the muzzle area appears shortened unlike a side on effect which reveals a long snout. To create the feeling of depth for the protruding muzzle, concentrate on the accuracy of the highlights and shadows.

MORGAN

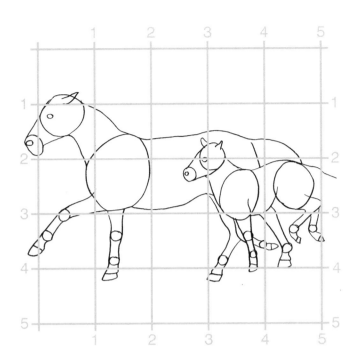

STEP 1:

On your own piece of paper, begin by very lightly drawing a twenty-five square grid using a ruler. A standard 2B pencil is ideal to draw basic circles and lines, as well as the main shapes of the finished sketch. Use the grid to help create accurate proportions.

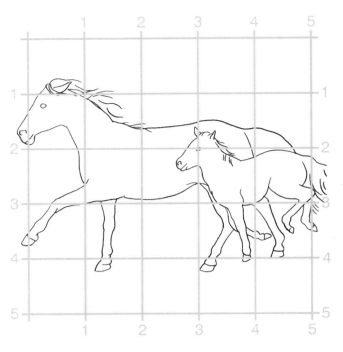

STEP 2:

Lightly sketching, follow the basic shapes you have just created and develop the outline of the image and its features. Still focusing on proportions and accuracy.

STEP 3:

When satisfied with your outlines, use an eraser to tidy any unnecessary lines or mistakes.

STEP 4:

Using a 4B and a 6B pencil to lightly render the image, copy the techniques shown in the example and read the observation details to help achieve an accurate result.

Sketching Animals

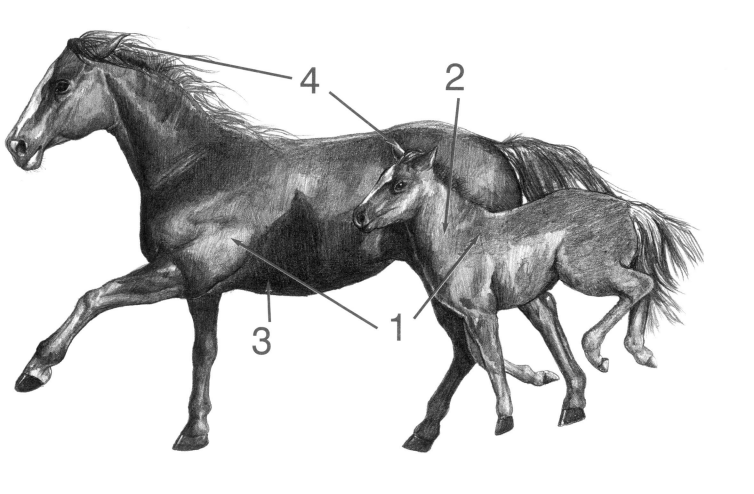

OBSERVATION DETAILS:

1. The foal's coat will differ from the mare's in that it should appear rough and fluffy compared to her sleek shiny finish. As such, the contrast is important and attention should be given to pencil shading. For the mother's coat the tip of the pencil should be used in most areas maintaining a consistent sleekness. The foal's coat requires the pencil to be turned sideways creating a rougher rendering.

2. The tone in which both horses are shaded is also important, as if colouring is too similar in density, blending into each other will lose individual effect. The foal should be a lighter colouring of the two.

3. The shadow falling across the mother's body is also vital in separating the two animals rendered heavily, it will make ske contrast stronger.

4. The ears of the mare and the foal indicate their constant communication, however subtle. Note that one ear of each is pointed towards the other, further confirming their union, even when galloping.

AMERICAN BISON

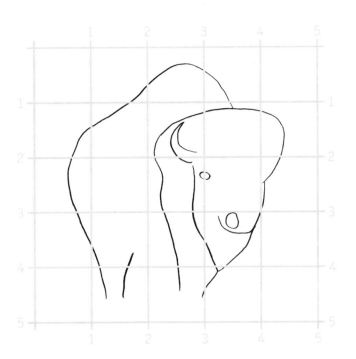

STEP 1:

On your own piece of paper, begin by very lightly drawing a twenty-five square grid using a ruler. A standard 2B pencil is ideal to draw basic circles and lines, as well as the main shapes of the finished sketch. Use the grid to help create accurate proportions.

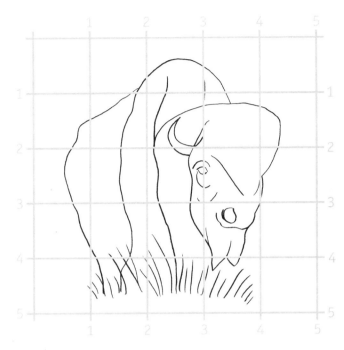

STEP 2:

Lightly sketching, follow the basic shapes already created and develop the outline of the image and its features. Still focusing on proportions and accuracy.

STEP 3:

When satisfied with your outlines, use an eraser to tidy any unnecessary lines or mistakes.

STEP 4:

Using a 4B and 6B pencil to lightly render the image, copy the techniques shown in the example and read the observation details to help achieve an accurate result.

Sketching Animals

OBSERVATION DETAILS:

1. The bison has long shaggy hair over its entire body. Using regular pencil strokes, make the hair as realistic as possible. Being aware of the varying lengths as in some cases they may appear as tufts.

2. Large areas of the body are dark. Therefore light upon the body is very important when illustrating different sections of both body and facial features.

3. As the bison's hooves are hidden under long hair, to increase the visual interest of the composition add grass at the base of the animal. This creates a platform and a setting for the bison, perhaps giving the early stages for a more expansive illustration showing further environment.

WEIMARANER

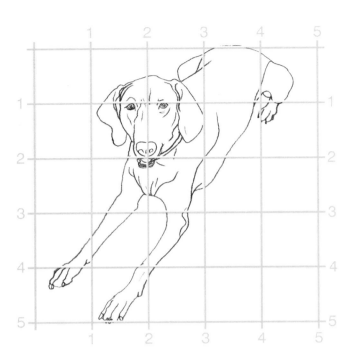

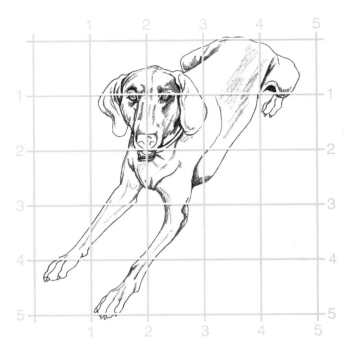

STEP 1:
On your own piece of paper, begin by very lightly drawing a twenty-five square grid using a ruler. A standard 2B pencil is ideal to draw basic circles and lines, as well as the main shapes of the finished sketch. Use the grid to help create accurate proportions.

STEP 2:
When satisfied with this outline stage, erase unnecessary lines or mistakes so your illustration is both neat and well-proportioned

STEP 3:
Using a 4B and a 6B pencil to lightly render the image, copy the techniques shown in the example and read the observation details to help achieve an accurate result.

Sketching Animals

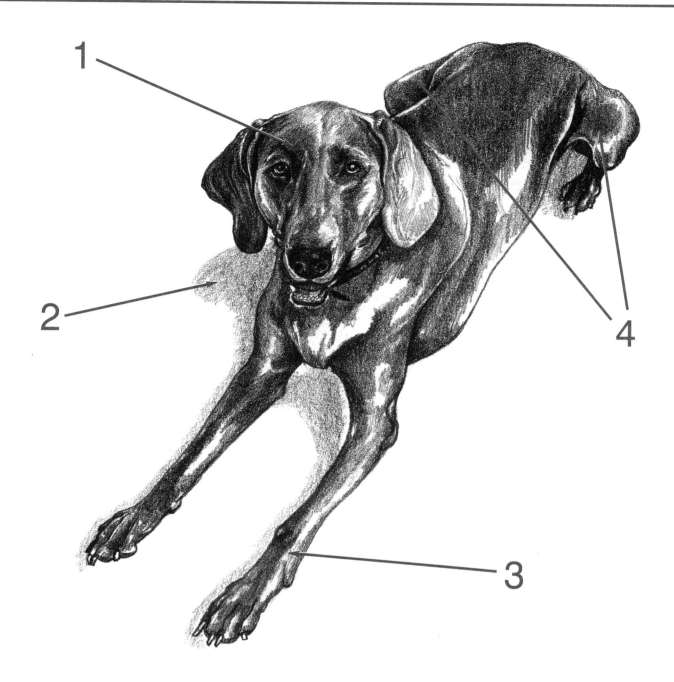

OBSERVATION DETAILS:

1. This dog has short and shiny hair, therefore the feature requires much more shading. Make an effort not to make the strokes too dark, as facial features and other necessary details can be lost.

2. Adding a shadow to the underside of the dog creates a base on which to lay, providing greater realism. Shadows should be drawn to the left, consistent with the light source. If unsure, place the shadows to the opposite side of highlighted features.

3. The front legs and paws will dramatically effect the whole perspective if drawn incorrectly. If alignment is difficult use your pencil to measure the length of the legs, comparing this to another part of the body. This will help achieve correct proportions and angles.

4. When laying down, hind legs are usually tucked underneath the body, revealing only the paws. The shape these hind quarters make is important in showing the muscles and the way the skin stretches when in this position.

WELSH PONY

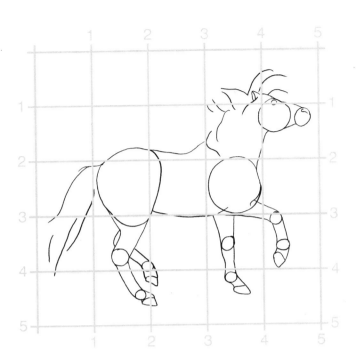

STEP 1:

On your own piece of paper, begin by very lightly drawing a twenty-five square grid using a ruler. A standard 2B pencil is ideal to draw basic circles and lines, as well as the main shapes of the finished sketch. Use the grid to help create accurate proportions.

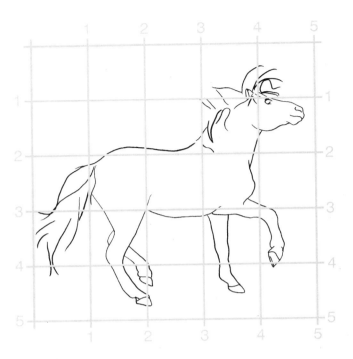

STEP 2:

Lightly sketching, follow the basic shapes you have just created and develop the outline of the image and its features. Still focusing on proportions and accuracy.

STEP 3:

When satisfied with your outlines, use an eraser to tidy any unnecessary lines or mistakes.

STEP 4:

Using a 4B and a 6B pencil to lightly render the image, copy the techniques shown in the example and read the observation details to help achieve an accurate result.

Sketching Animals

OBSERVATION DETAILS:

1. The Welsh pony is a frisky character and in his case, the mane is flicked proudly in the air as he prances about. Pencil strokes should be made loosely and erratically in order to portray the stray hair in motion.

2. When drawing the horse's legs note the prominence of muscles and tendons for the different poses. In this composition they become a feature, particularly as the sunlight falls across the body.

3. The way in which the hooves are drawn can also contribute to the success of the illustration. Although only a small part of the body they can have a large impact on the accuracy of a sketch. Note the way they rest on the ground and the angles created when legs are bent.

4. The strongly shadowed areas can be useful in defining the body mass and enhancing dimension. Quite naturally they lead the eye to highlighted areas upon the horse's body, so care needs be taken with detailing.

Sketching Animals

POLAR BEAR

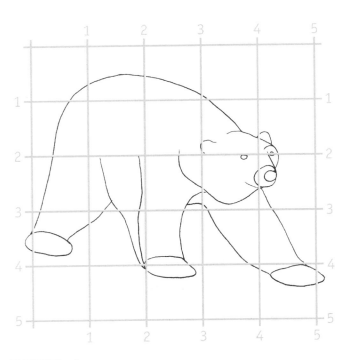

STEP 1:

On your own piece of paper, begin by very lightly drawing a twenty-five square grid using a ruler. A standard 2B pencil is ideal to draw basic circles and lines, as well as the main shapes of the finished sketch. Use the grid to help create accurate proportions.

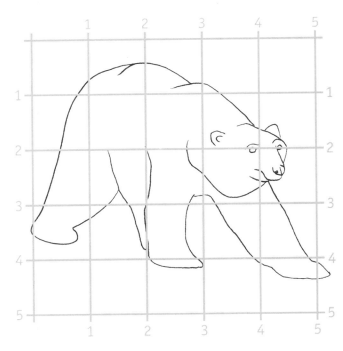

STEP 2:

Lightly sketching, follow the basic shapes already created and develop the outline of the image and its features. Still focusing on proportions and accuracy.

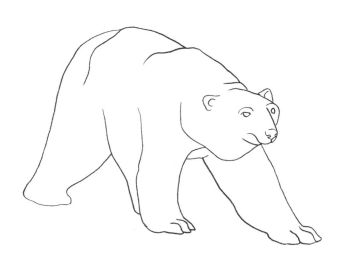

STEP 3:

When satisfied with your outlines, use an eraser to tidy any unnecessary lines or mistakes.

STEP 4:

Using a 4B and 6B pencil to lightly render the image, copy the techniques shown in the example and read the observation details to help achieve an accurate result.

Sketching Animals

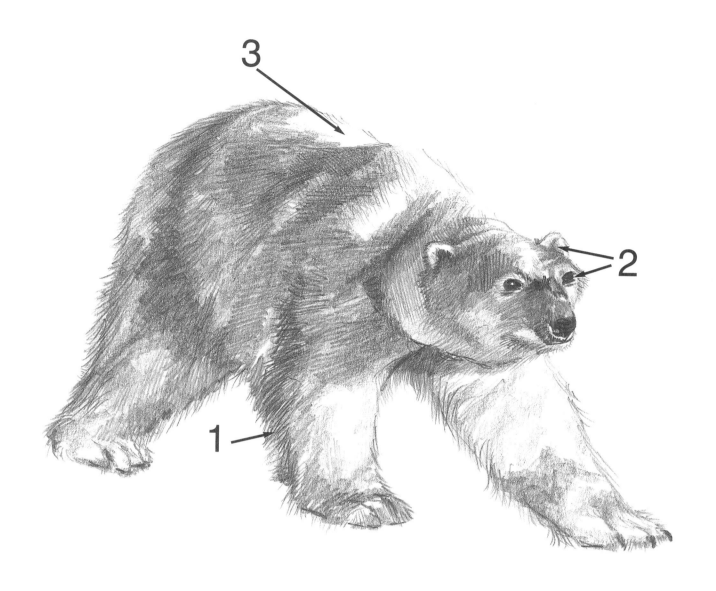

OBSERVATION DETAILS:

1. In this composition, the polar bear's hind leg is hidden behind the front. Without letting this hidden leg blend into the front one as the effect can become visually confusing. It is recommended you render the hind leg darker than the front.

2. The shape of the polar bear's head is distinctly different to other bears. Attention should be paid where the eyes and ears fall in relation to all other features.

3. The polar bear's body is extensively shadowed due to the direction of the light source. Unwarrented heavy shading reduces body curves and creases, becoming almost impossible without emphasis on muscle tonings.

AIREDALE TERRIER

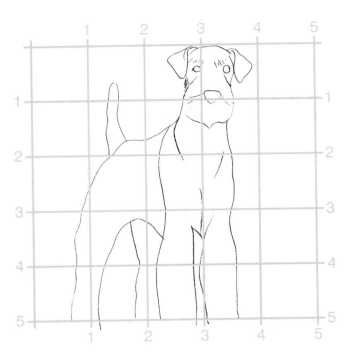

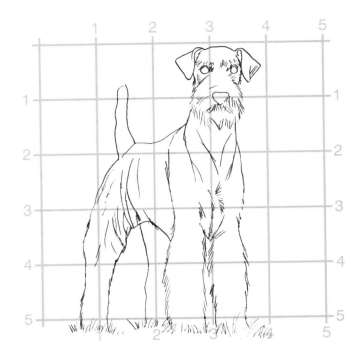

STEP 1:

On your own piece of paper, begin by very lightly drawing a twenty-five square grid using a ruler. A standard 2B pencil is ideal to draw basic circles and lines, as well as the main shapes of the finished sketch. Use the grid to help create accurate proportions.

STEP 2:

When satisfied with this outline stage, erase unnecessary lines or mistakes so your illustration is both neat and well-proportioned.

STEP 3:

Using a 4B and a 6B pencil to lightly render the image, copy the techniques shown in the example and read the observation details to help achieve an accurate result.

Sketching Animals

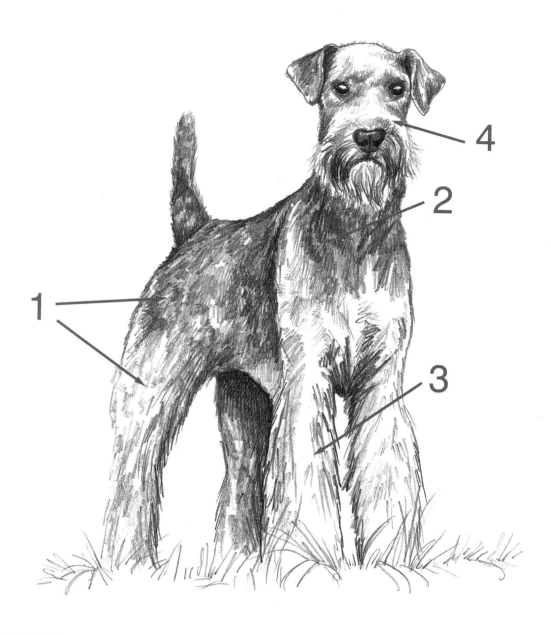

OBSERVATION DETAILS:

1. The Airedale's coat has coarse wavy fur. Create texture by using a sketchy style in these sections which will avoid the appearance of smoother shading.

2. The skin around the chest and neck is loose. Shading here should still be sketchy, but considerably darker.

3. The legs have long hair covering them, hiding their true shape. As this hair is bulky and quite long, shade in the areas of shadow only, avoiding the appearance of a large grey mass.

4. The top of the muzzle needs to be prominent against the rest of the face, giving dimension.

PERUVIAN PASO

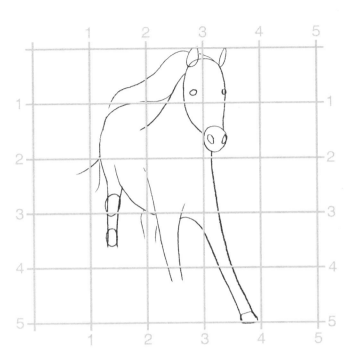

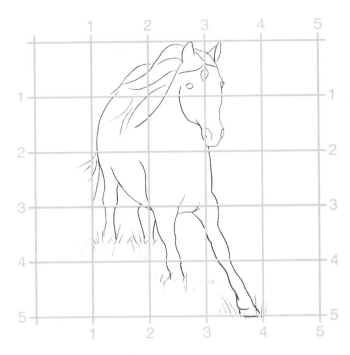

STEP 1:

On your own piece of paper, begin by very lightly drawing a twenty-five square grid using a ruler. A standard 2B pencil is ideal to draw basic circles and lines, as well as the main shapes of the finished sketch. Use the grid to help create accurate proportions.

STEP 2:

Lightly sketching, follow the basic shapes you have just created and develop the outline of the image and its features. Still focusing on proportions and accuracy.

STEP 3:

When satisfied with your outlines, use an eraser to tidy any unnecessary lines or mistakes.

STEP 4:

Using a 4B and a 6B pencil to lightly render the image, copy the techniques shown in the example and read the observation details to help achieve an accurate result.

Sketching Animals

OBSERVATION DETAILS:

1. In this feature the grass should be drawn in line, therefore not detracting from the horse in motion, of course being the main focal point of the illustration.

2. The reduction in size of the horse's body on this angle can be a challenge when achieving accurate perspective. Attention must be given here to achieve accuracy and perceived movement.

3. Not all details need to be drawn to finish an illustration. By omiting the hooves in this piece and introducing the pasture grass it allows the audience to imagine the horse pounding through long grass, rather than across a bare page.

KOALA

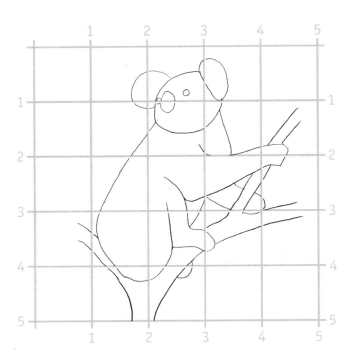

STEP 1:

On your own piece of paper, begin by very lightly drawing a twenty-five square grid using a ruler. A standard 2B pencil is ideal to draw basic circles and lines, as well as the main shapes of the finished sketch. Use the grid to help create accurate proportions.

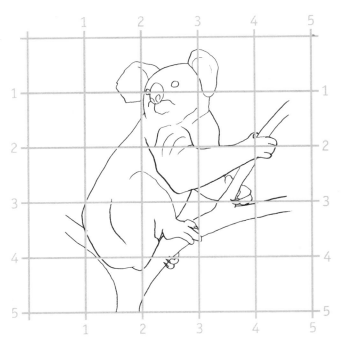

STEP 2:

Lightly sketching, follow the basic shapes already created and develop the outline of the image and its features. Still focusing on proportions and accuracy.

STEP 3:

When satisfied with your outlines, use an eraser to tidy any unnecessary lines or mistakes.

STEP 4:

Using a 4B and 6B pencil to lightly render the image, copy the techniques shown in the example and read the observation details to help achieve an accurate result.

Sketching Animals

OBSERVATION DETAILS:

1. The ears of the koala are very fluffy and quite round. Pencil strokes should reflect this, especially along the edges. Flicking gently only with the pencil to create this effect, because pressing too firmly is not recommended. Perhaps practise on a separate piece of paper until the style is perfected.

2. The fur falls into layers especially along the arms and shoulders and these patterns should be varied in their intensity. Locating thicker lines which form the creases of the body, these will be darker and are most important, controlling the form of the koala and making the pose more realistic.

3. The koala's bottom follows the line of the tree. Consequently there should not be a gap between the koala and the branch. The bottom of the koala is fluffy and soft and melds into the crook of the tree.

BULLDOG

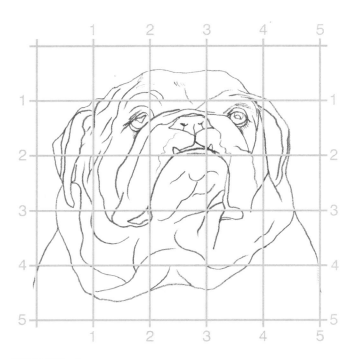

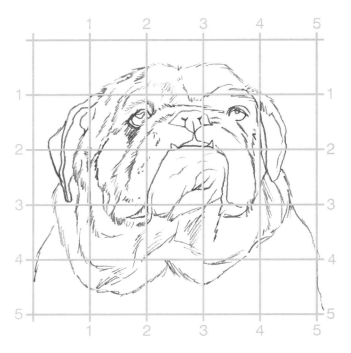

STEP 1:

On your own piece of paper, begin by very lightly drawing a twenty-five square grid using a ruler. A standard 2B pencil is ideal to draw basic circles and lines, as well as the main shapes of the finished sketch. Use the grid to help create accurate proportions.

STEP 2:

When satisfied with this outline stage, erase unnecessary lines or mistakes so your illustration is both neat and well-proportioned.

STEP 3:

Using a 4B and a 6B pencil to lightly render the image, copy the techniques shown in the example and read the observation details to help achieve an accurate result.

Sketching Animals

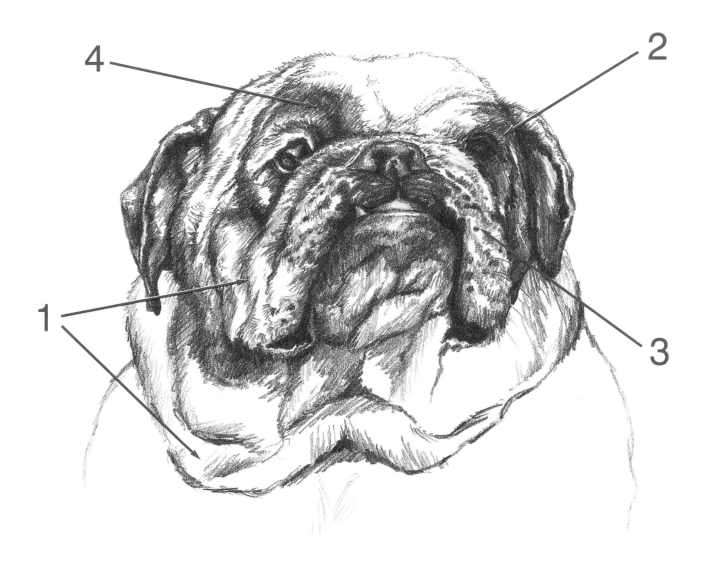

OBSERVATION DETAILS:

1. Characteristically the bulldog has very loose skin and appears "floppy" around the face and chest. This must be recreated accurately as it is a strong feature, revealing his personality and recognisable facial characteristics.

2. The second eye falls behind shadow, however there should still be definition to it. Try not to lose any details by shading too strongly over the top. Draw the basic shapes to begin with, then shade to acknowledge markings and lighting.

3. The Bulldog has a significant number of pronounced dimples where the whiskers belong. As his skin is droopy, these spots can be drawn roughly and should form vague lines when getting closer to the nose region, although spaced further down the jowls.

4. As with the Pug, focus on the dark patches around the eyes, use them to enhance the facial features. They can become tools of expression, as the eyebrows do on a human, with the shape raised slightly at the peak and slightly exaggerated.

FRIESIAN

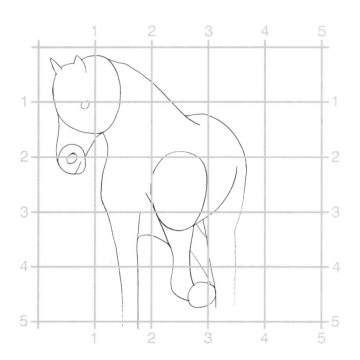

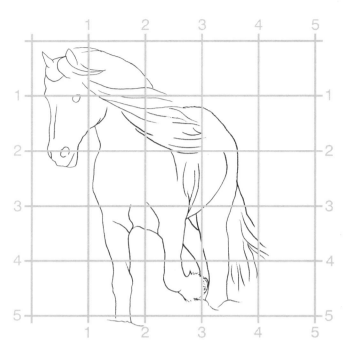

STEP 1:

On your own piece of paper, begin by very lightly drawing a twenty-five square grid using a ruler. A standard 2B pencil is ideal to draw basic circles and lines, as well as the main shapes of the finished sketch. Use the grid to help create accurate proportions.

STEP 2:

Lightly sketching, follow the basic shapes you have just created and develop the outline of the image and its features. Still focusing on proportions and accuracy.

STEP 3:

When satisfied with your outlines, use an eraser to tidy any unnecessary lines or mistakes.

STEP 4:

Using a 4B and a 6B pencil to lightly render the image, copy the techniques shown in the example and read the observation details to help achieve an accurate result.

OBSERVATION DETAILS:

1. The form of the Friesian needs to be strong and sturdy with detail given to the light source falling upon the muscles. The coat being black, reflections become more important in accurately recreating muscle structure and body mass.

2. Leaving highlights almost white with only slight shading along the edges where they bleed into the black coat. These edges need to be shaded, alternatively the highlights will appear as patches of colour on the coat.

3. By adding a simple background the horse is no longer 'floating in air' and gives the viewer more feeling toward generated motion, when galloping. This, together with the great force with which his hooves are hitting the ground, confirm the prowess and great strength of this breed.

HARP SEAL

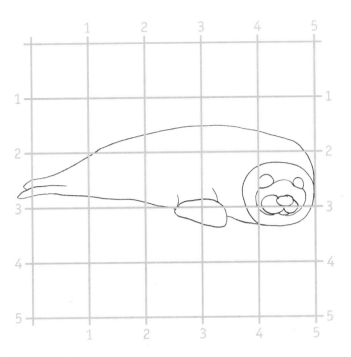

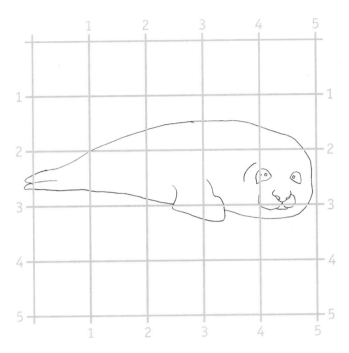

STEP 1:

On your own piece of paper, begin by very lightly drawing a twenty-five square grid using a ruler. A standard 2B pencil is ideal to draw basic circles and lines, as well as the main shapes of the finished sketch. Use the grid to help create accurate proportions.

STEP 2:

Lightly sketching, follow the basic shapes already created and develop the outline of the image and its features. Still focusing on proportions and accuracy.

STEP 3:

When satisfied with your outlines, use an eraser to tidy any unnecessary lines or mistakes.

STEP 4:

Using a 4B and 6B pencil to lightly render the image, copy the techniques shown in the example and read the observation details to help achieve an accurate result.

Sketching Animals

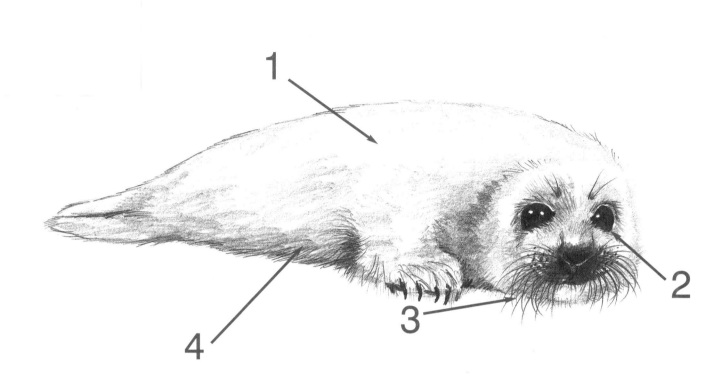

1

2

3

4

OBSERVATION DETAILS:

1. The majority of the young seal's coat is white. Therefore a careful study of shaded areas will be emphasised with lightly shaded areas only. Leave the highlighted sections along the top of the body without any shading.

2. The seal's eyes are black and require the use of a 6B pencil. Reflections are vital giving them life, mark where they will fall and shade around them.

3. Whiskers should be sharp and precisely drawn. Sharpen your pencil to a point, then make strong even strokes in a downward curve. Vary the strokes enabling some to overlap others, but not too heavily. Then to create the tapered ends, gently flick the pencil.

4. Edges of the seal's fur needs to give the feeling of fluffiness and density. Drawing along these edges in soft strokes, follow the direction of the coat. Keep it fainter near the head where very careful shading is more important.

BULL TERRIER

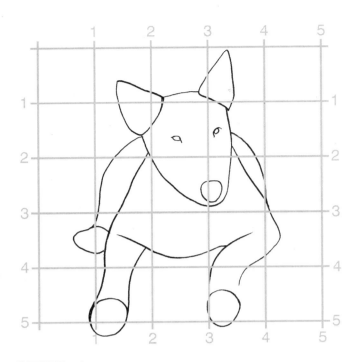

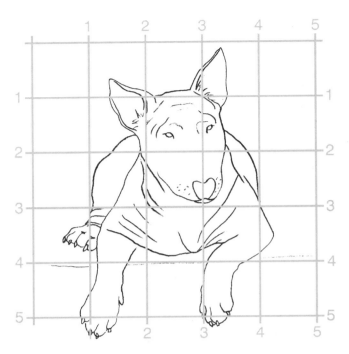

STEP 1:

On your own piece of paper, begin by very lightly drawing a twenty-five square grid using a ruler. A standard 2B pencil is ideal to draw basic circles and lines, as well as the main shapes of the finished sketch. Use the grid to help create accurate proportions.

STEP 2:

When satisfied with this outline stage, erase unnecessary lines or mistakes so your illustration is both neat and well-proportioned.

STEP 3:

Using a 4B and a 6B pencil to lightly render the image, copy the techniques shown in the example and read the observation details to help achieve an accurate result.

Sketching Animals

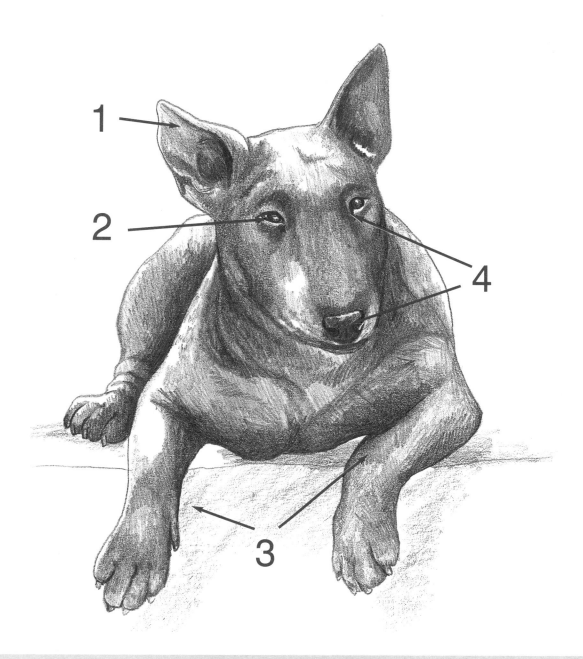

OBSERVATION DETAILS:

1. The Bull Terrier has quite large pointy ears. When detailing these it is most important that the correct proportion to the head is maintained.

2. The eyes appear small and squinty and you may find it difficult giving them expression. Use the eyebrows and surrounding areas of the eyes to show the strength of character.

3. This composition has legs and paws dangling over a ledge, giving the viewer another perspective. Relaxed poses can often be more interesting than standing or sitting. It may also be more challenging when showing some limbs whilst others are hidden from view. In these instances both muscles and body shape will change accordingly.

4. The darkest parts of this illustration should be the eyes and nose. Avoid rendering the rest of the body too heavily.

SADDELBRED

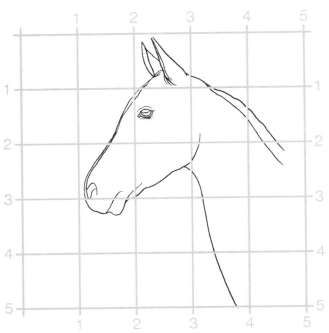

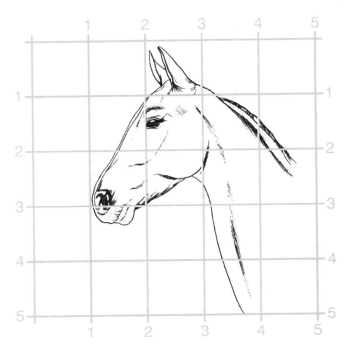

STEP 1:

On your own piece of paper, begin by very lightly drawing a twenty-five square grid using a ruler. A standard 2B pencil is ideal to draw basic circles and lines, as well as the main shapes of the finished sketch. Use the grid to help create accurate proportions.

STEP 2:

When satisfied with this outline stage, erase unnecessary lines or mistakes so that your illustration is both neat and well-proportioned.

STEP 3:

Using a 4B and a 6B pencil to lightly render the image, copy the techniques shown in the example and read the observation details to help achieve an accurate result.

Sketching Animals

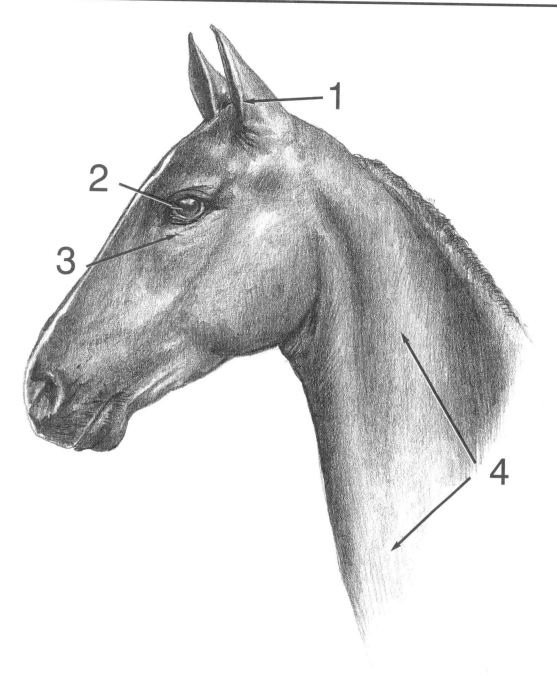

OBSERVATION DETAILS:

1. The Saddlebred has an aristocratic look to the head and facial features. The ears must be drawn pricked-up and alert.

2. The eyes evoke thoughtful expression and should capture the viewers interest. Avoid rendering the eye region too heavily. Reflections must be prominent, as should the white of the eye.

3. Small details can make all the difference in creating a realistic portrait. Note the subtle wrinkles of skin around the ears, eyes and muzzle.

4. The coat is smooth and neat and will be appropriately shown by effective pencil strokes. The rendering needs to be gradually reduced towards the end of the neck and irregular in parts to create interest.

RINGTAIL POSSUM

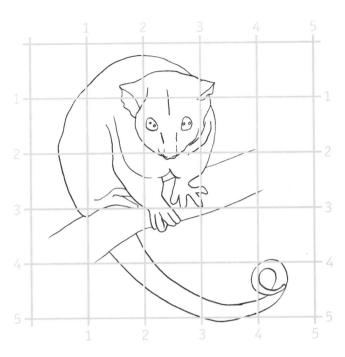

STEP 1:

On your own piece of paper, begin by very lightly drawing a twenty-five square grid using a ruler. A standard 2B pencil is ideal to draw basic circles and lines, as well as the main shapes of the finished sketch. Use the grid to help create accurate proportions.

STEP 2:

Lightly sketching, follow the basic shapes already created and develop the outline of the image and its features. Still focusing on proportions and accuracy.

STEP 3:

When satisfied with your outlines, use an eraser to tidy any unnecessary lines or mistakes.

STEP 4:

Using a 4B and 6B pencil to lightly render the image, copy the techniques shown in the example and read the observation details to help achieve an accurate result.

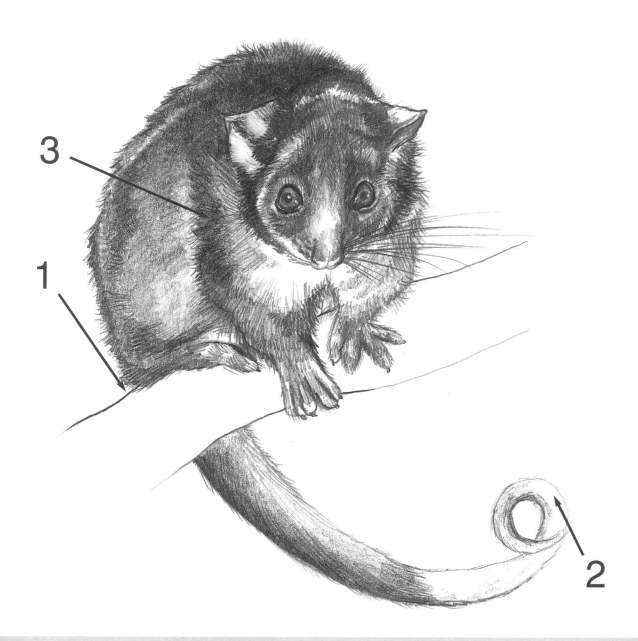

OBSERVATION DETAILS:

1. The branch the possum is holding on to can be left in line only. Contrasting with the heavy shading of the possum's body and making the animal more outstanding as an art piece.

2. The tail curving at the bottom should be left white, consistent with the marsupials' common markings. Apply a little shading to the shadows, giving dimension, especially where the tail curls.

3. The fur is quite fluffy and dark. Use the side of your 6B pencil, shading lightly at first, then building texture as necessary.

DACHSHUND

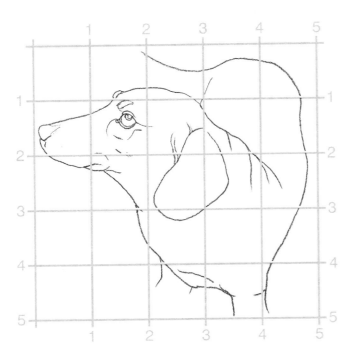

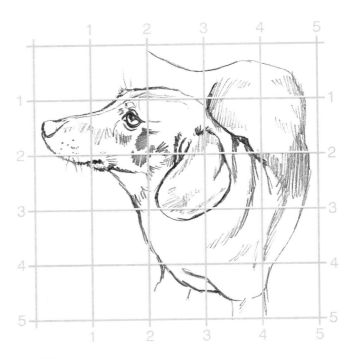

STEP 1:
On your own piece of paper, begin by very lightly drawing a twenty-five square grid using a ruler. A standard 2B pencil is ideal to draw basic circles and lines, as well as the main shapes of the finished sketch. Use the grid to help create accurate proportions.

STEP 2:
When satisfied with this outline stage, erase unnecessary lines or mistakes so your illustration is both neat and well-proportioned.

STEP 3:
Using a 4B and a 6B pencil to lightly render the image, copy the techniques shown in the example and read the observation details to help achieve an accurate result.

Sketching Animals

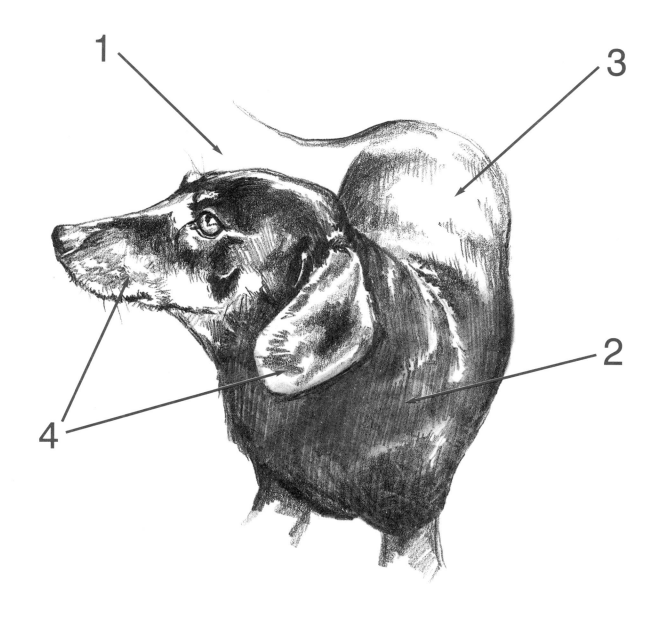

OBSERVATION DETAILS:

1. This composition is particularly appealing because it leaves only a suggestion as to the body shape. Yet it captures the main characteristics such as the short, long body and tiny legs. The tail is a tapered line giving the viewer the idea as to positioning only. Drawing a single sketched line also enhances the feeling of movement as the tail wags.

2. The fur of the Dachshund is relatively dark and will require the use of a 6B pencil, achieving a   smooth and even shading.

3. The reflections and shiny nature of the coat should be shown by leaving white within the shading. This then creates a stark contrast. 6B pencils are very soft and therefore preferred, although care must be taken with rendering. To avoid any smudging, use a clean piece of paper over artwork, on which you rest your hand.

4. The Dachshund has a very long muzzle and rounded ears. Proper results will not be achieved if these features are an incorrect length.

PONY OF THE AMERICAS

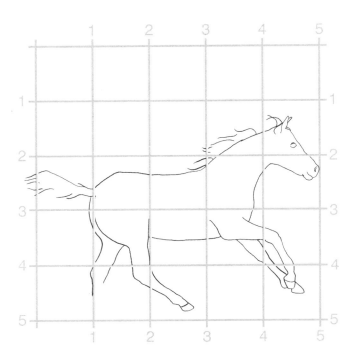

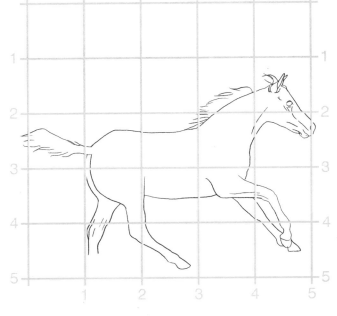

STEP 1:

On your own piece of paper, begin by very lightly drawing a twenty-five square grid using a ruler. A standard 2B pencil is ideal to draw basic circles and lines, as well as the main shapes of the finished sketch. Use the grid to help create accurate proportions.

STEP 2:

When satisfied with this outline stage, erase unnecessary lines or mistakes so that your illustration is both neat and well-proportioned.

STEP 4:

Using a 4B and a 6B pencil to lightly render the image, copy the techniques shown in the example and read the observation details to help achieve an accurate result.

Sketching Animals

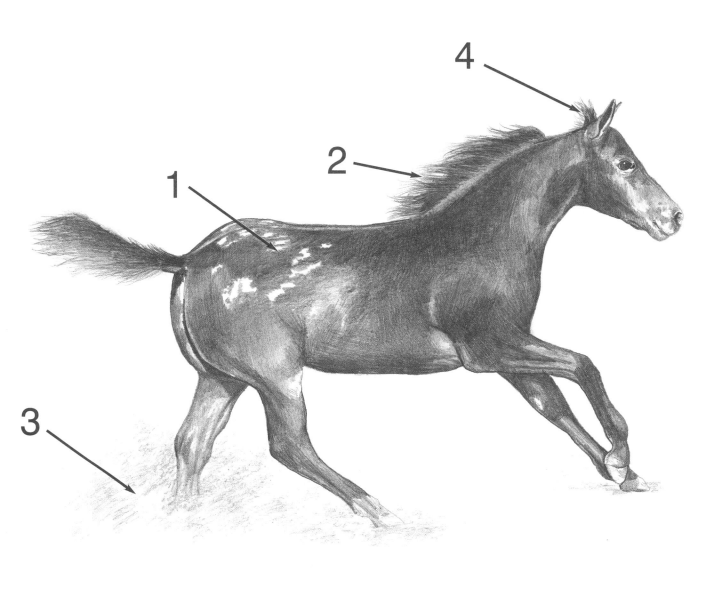

OBSERVATION DETAILS:

1. The light spots upon the rump contrast with the dark coat of the horse and should be conspicuous and impactful. Render as little as possible in these whiter areas.

2. A flowing mane and tail always makes a drawing very satisfying. In this case, they both flow in the same direction, giving the audience the illusion of speed and a feeling for the motion of the travelling horse.

3. Emphasising the movement we show small sections of sand and dirt being flung up around and behind the hooves and legs, once again the focus is on speed and power, for which all horses are noted. The shadow beneath gives the composition depth.

4. The ears are to be drawn forward, pricked and alert with flared nostrils, whilst the calm expression of the eye reflects a relaxed disposition. The composition is perfectly balanced with an easy flowing line from the head and body to the tip of the tail.

DEER

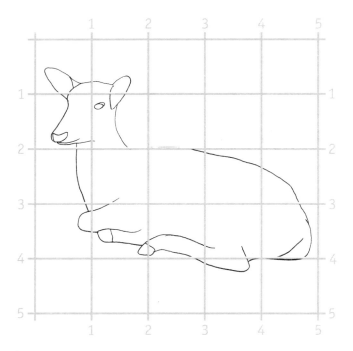

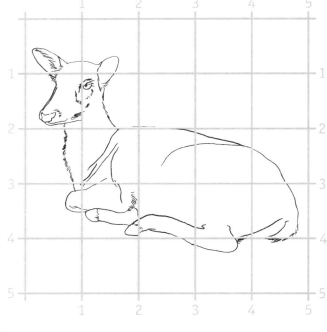

STEP 1:

On your own piece of paper, begin by very lightly drawing a twenty-five square grid using a ruler. A standard 2B pencil is ideal to draw basic circles and lines, as well as the main shapes of the finished sketch. Use the grid to help create accurate proportions.

STEP 2:

When satisfied with this outline stage, erase unnecessary lines or mistakes so that your illustration is both neat and well-proportioned.

STEP 3:

Use a 4B and a 6B pencil to lightly render the deer. Copy the techniques shown in the example and read the observation details to help achieve an accurate result.

Sketching Animals

OBSERVATION DETAILS:

1. The spots on the deer's body are not rendered, but instead are left to show the whiteness of the paper background. Avoid outlining these spots before shading their surrounds. Create as you proceed by carefully examining the above illustration. This will finish as a more realistic effect of fur.

2. Note the way in which the deer has muscles and bones protruding from the bulk of the body when in a laying position. These details ensure more accurate perspective and composition, keeping the body in proportion and alertness.

3. Similarly to that of the kangaroo, the ears and eyes should be drawn alert and facing a particular spot, therefore increasing the keen expression.

4. The main focal point for this illustration is the head, together with its spots along the top of its body. The stomach region, legs and tail can be rendered with minimal coverage.

PEKINGESE

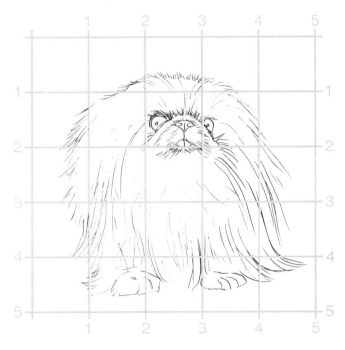

STEP 1:

On your own piece of paper, begin by very lightly drawing a twenty-five square grid using a ruler. A standard 2B pencil is ideal to draw basic circles and lines, as well as the main shapes of the finished sketch. Use the grid to help create accurate proportions.

STEP 2:

When satisfied with this outline stage, erase unnecessary lines or mistakes so your illustration is both neat and well-proportioned.

STEP 3:

Using a 4B and a 6B pencil to lightly render the image, copy the techniques shown in the example and read the observation details to help achieve an accurate result.

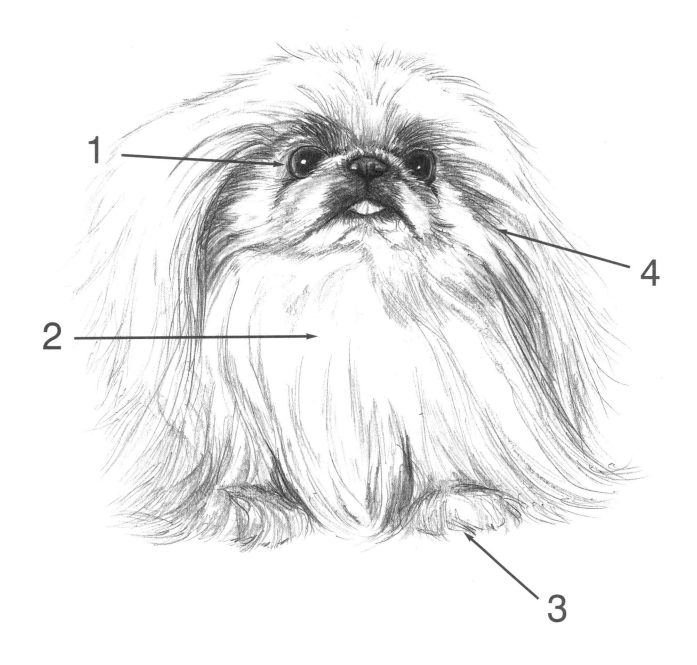

OBSERVATION DETAILS:

1. The Pekingese is a funny little character and great attention needs to be taken to correctly show the facial features, in particular the eyes, being the main focal point:

2. The bulk of the Pekingese's fur should be left white with the only rendering shown to areas of shadow revealing the direction of the flowing hair.

3. The paws are tucked underneath the hair and should not be drawn too conspicuously. They should blend in, particularly as they are heavily haired as well. However they need to appear separate from the chest area. This can be achieved through pencil strokes, making certain the direction of your shading is executed in a curved motion revealing the roundness of the paws

4. Similar to the Afghan Hound, the Pekingese's ears are barely noticeable amongst the bulk of the head and body hair. The shadows will also become important in showing the length and presence of the ears.

WALER

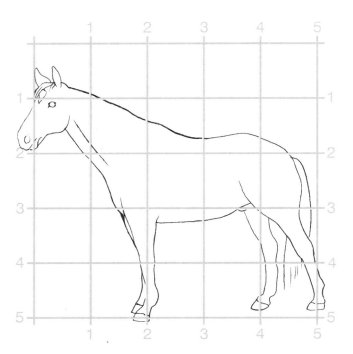

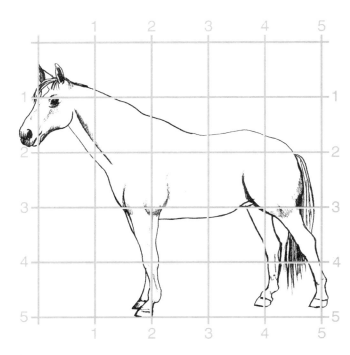

STEP 1:

On your own piece of paper, begin by very lightly drawing a twenty-five square grid using a ruler. A standard 2B pencil is ideal to draw basic circles and lines, as well as the main shapes of the finished sketch. Use the grid to help create accurate proportions.

STEP 2:

When satisfied with this outline stage, erase unnecessary lines or mistakes so that your illustration is both neat and well-proportioned.

STEP 3:

Using a 4B and a 6B pencil to lightly render the image, copy the techniques shown in the example and read the observation details to help achieve an accurate result.

Sketching Animals

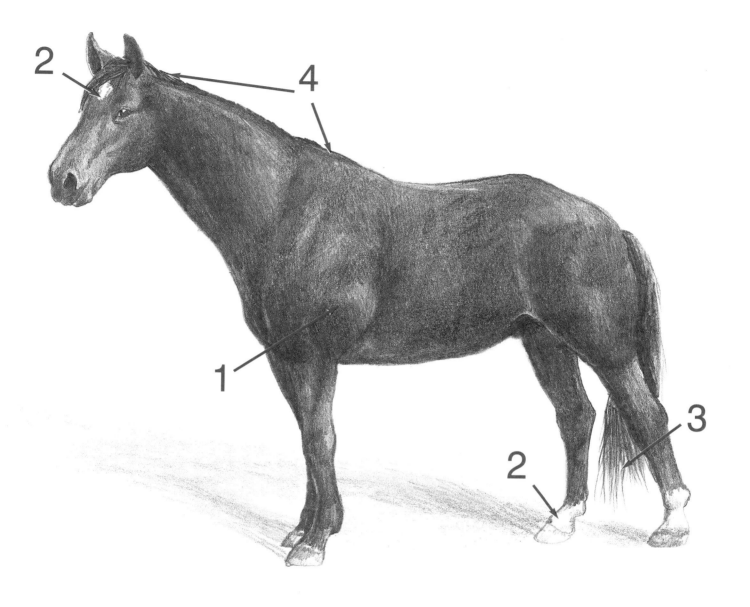

OBSERVATION DETAILS:

1. When drawing in pencil, reflections of light upon muscle become extremely important, assisting in the depiction of shape and form.

2. As this horse has a dark body, the white areas, such as the star between the eyes and the socks above the hooves, must be obvious. These create a welcome contrast to the rest of the body.

3. The tail hair is quite long, hanging loosely behind the hindquarters and is straight, not wavy.

4. The line along the top of the body is important when showing both a streamlined a style together with correct proportions.

CHIMPANZEE

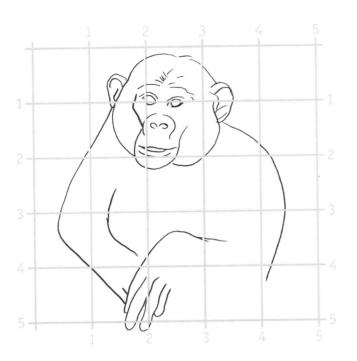

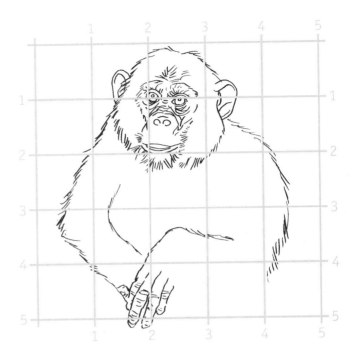

STEP 1:

On your own piece of paper, begin by very lightly drawing a twenty-five square grid using a ruler. A standard 2B pencil is ideal to draw basic circles and lines, as well as the main shapes of the finished sketch. Use the grid to help create accurate proportions.

STEP 2:

When satisfied with this outline stage, erase unnecessary lines or mistakes so that your illustration is both neat and well-proportioned.

STEP 3:

Use a 4B and a 6B pencil to lightly render the chimpanzee. Copy the techniques shown in the example and read the observation details to help achieve an accurate result.

Sketching Animals

OBSERVATION DETAILS:

1. The fur on the chimp's body can be drawn in a sketchy manner, varying the pencil strokes and making it appear to move in different directions. At the same time altering the length will ensure a more realistic feature.

2. The chimp's pose in this illustration does not require including the rest of the body. Compositions such as this are enhanced by features represented which would normally be lost if the entire animal was drawn. Both hands and the facial expressions alter the mood and tell more about character and emotion.

3. As most of the chimp's body hair is black, areas of highlight become very important. Equally the arms are significant to the composition as they have areas of white showing through to contrast the darkness of the head.

4. Take care not to shade the face too heavily as the eyes and nose areas once again reveal personality and emotions, a most significant attraction when drawing with a creature having such creative characteristics.

SILKY TERRIER

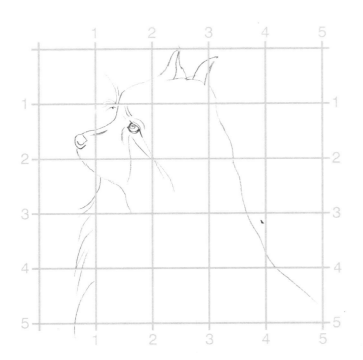

STEP 1:

On your own piece of paper, begin by very lightly drawing a twenty-five square grid using a ruler. A standard 2B pencil is ideal to draw basic circles and lines, as well as the main shapes of the finished sketch. Use the grid to help create accurate proportions.

STEP 2:

When satisfied with this outline stage, erase unnecessary lines or mistakes so your illustration is both neat and well-proportioned.

STEP 3:

Using a 4B and a 6B pencil to lightly render the image, copy the techniques shown in the example and read the observation details to help achieve an accurate result.

Sketching Animals

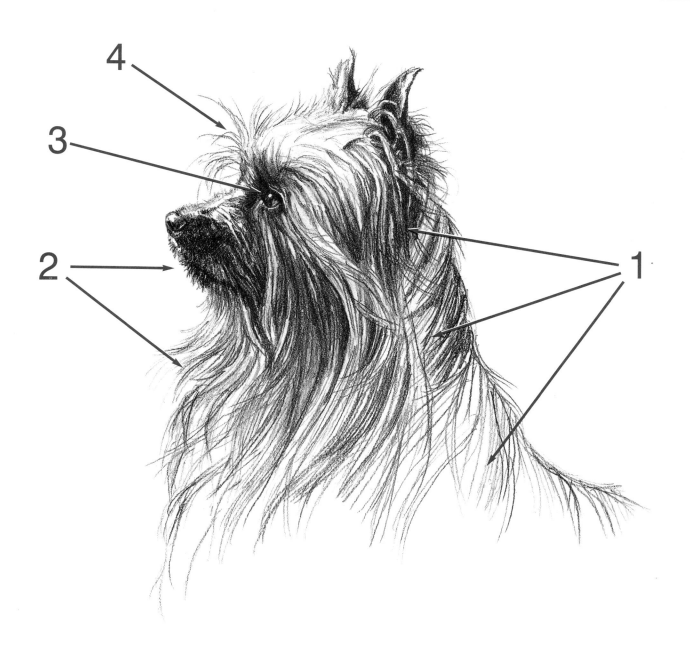

OBSERVATION DETAILS:

1. The hair patterns need not be overly shaded. Over shading will leave the hair looking dull and heavy rather than lively and wispy. Identify the areas of shadow and light, as well as the direction in which the hair flows, only drawing the most significant strands.

2. Keep all the whiskers on the muzzle very delicate and soft. Using light flicks of a sharpened 2B pencil, otherwise the strokes will be too thick. The main aim, to keep the strokes softer and tapering at the tips.

3. Reflection of light on the eyes is very important. Without this, the eyes become lost in shadows and appear dull and lifeless. Before shading the eye, draw the shape of the reflection, then shade the surround.

4. The hair overhanging and strands above the brow, draws the viewers attention to the eye. These hairs should be featured accurately and with a sharp pencil.

QUARTER HORSE

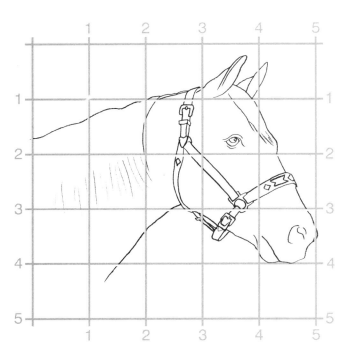

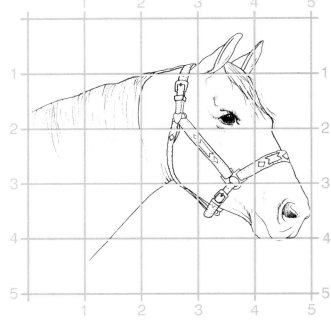

STEP 1:

On your own piece of paper, begin by very lightly drawing a twenty-five square grid using a ruler. A standard 2B pencil is ideal to draw basic circles and lines, as well as the main shapes of the finished sketch. Use the grid to help create accurate proportions.

STEP 2:

When satisfied with this outline stage, erase unnecessary lines or mistakes so that your illustration is both neat and well-proportioned

STEP 3:

Using a 4B and a 6B pencil to lightly render the image, copy the techniques shown in the example and read the observation details to help achieve an accurate result.

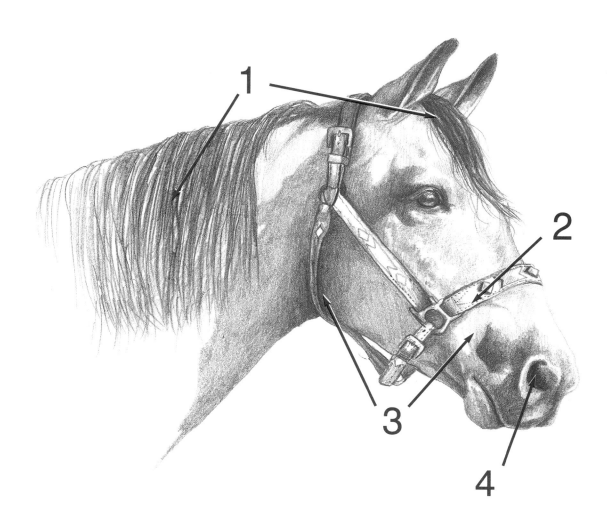

OBSERVATION DETAILS:

1. The mane falls half to one side of the neck with a small section to the opposite side and the front. This variation is more interesting and enhances the character of the horse.

2. The detail on the head halter gives an American West feel which reflects one of the areas this horse excels, Western riding. By adding details significant to the subject, the portrait reveals more interest and further talking points.

3. The light falls upon the face and highlights the nostrils and prominent areas. Understandably the shadows fall in areas of depression and around the neck.

4. The darkest aspects of the portrait, however, should be areas of deepest shadow, such as inside the ears and nostrils.

Sketching Animals

JAGUAR

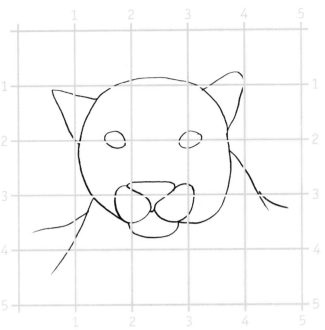

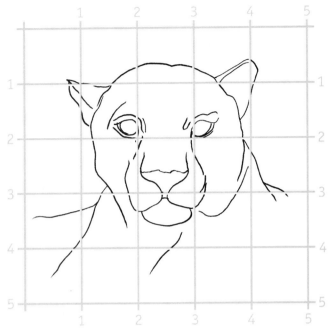

STEP 1:

On your own piece of paper, begin by very lightly drawing a twenty-five square grid using a ruler. A standard 2B pencil is ideal to draw basic circles and lines, as well as the main shapes of the finished sketch. Use the grid to help create accurate proportions.

STEP 2:

When satisfied with this outline stage, erase unnecessary lines or mistakes so that your illustration is both neat and well-proportioned

STEP 3:

Use a 4B and a 6B pencil to lightly render the jaguar. Copy the techniques shown in the example and read the observation details to help achieve an accurate result.

Sketching Animals

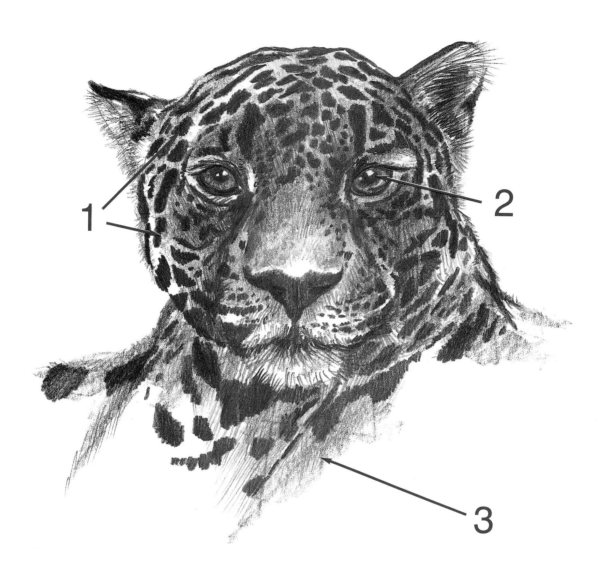

OBSERVATION DETAILS:

1. Spots on the jaguar's coat are irregular and each takes a different form. Avoid using similar patterns, tempting as it might be. Rendering needs to follow the form of the head as it curves. Equally the direction of the fur must be observed to help add dimension to your drawing.

2. The eyes are important as they should stare directly at the viewer. The jaguar is a hunter and this pose is typical, showing a feeling of confidence and power. Placement of the reflections is important. If executed incorrectly, they can make the animal's eyes appear cross-eyed or disproportionate.

3. The jaguar's throat and chest can be drawn in a sketchy style and should fade, adding edges to give a well-balanced composition, whilst concentrating the viewer's attention to the face.

SIBERIAN HUSKY

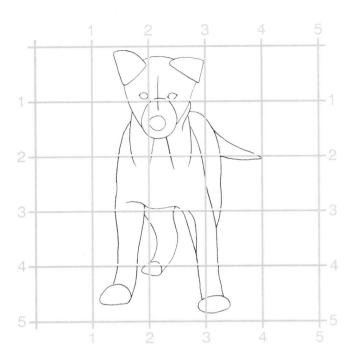

STEP 1:

On your own piece of paper, begin by very lightly drawing a twenty-five square grid using a ruler. A standard 2B pencil is ideal to draw basic circles and lines, as well as the main shapes of the finished sketch. Use the grid to help create accurate proportions.

STEP 2:

When satisfied with this outline stage, erase unnecessary lines or mistakes so your illustration is both neat and well-proportioned.

STEP 3:

Using a 4B and a 6B pencil to lightly render the image, copy the techniques shown in the example and read the observation details to help achieve an accurate result.

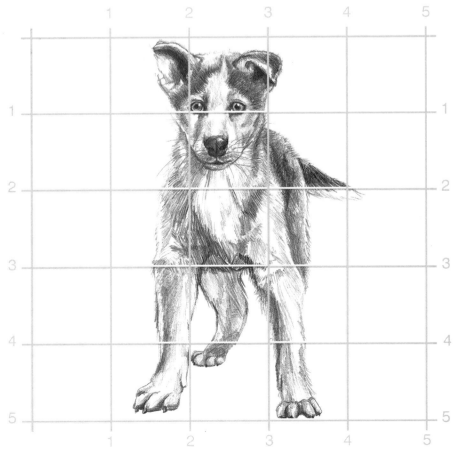

Sketching Animals

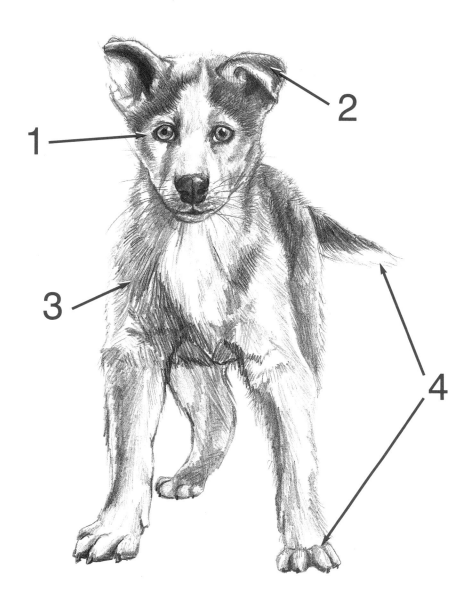

OBSERVATION DETAILS:

1. The eyes of the Husky are particularly important characteristics of this breed. Draw with great care, as they are the focal point of the piece, and the viewer should be drawn to them. The centre of the eye is darkest with the outer surface needing almost no shading at all. Reflections need to remain white and create the illusion of wetness.

2. As this dog is a puppy, the ears have not yet developed with full strength. Note how one ear bends forward with the other straight. Neither are yet pointed as with a mature Siberian Husky.

3. The coat is thick and straight and should be roughly drawn, yet with pencil strokes flowing in the one direction for the hair.

4. Dog paws are quite often seen at an angle as shown in this illustration. Training your eye to notice these differences is valuable, in not only main parts of the body but also smaller aspects such as; ears, tail, paws, nose. These will greatly influence realism and overall success of the representation.

PALOMINO

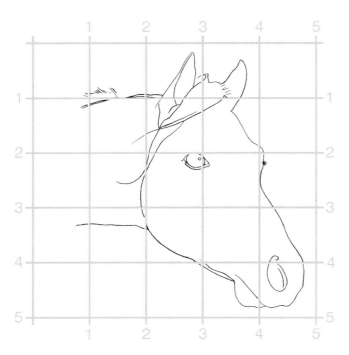

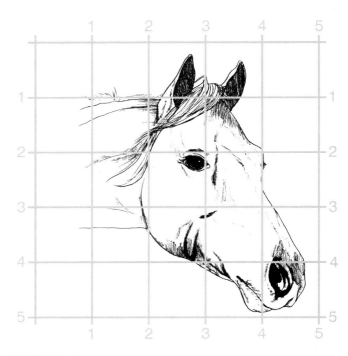

STEP 1:

On your own piece of paper, begin by very lightly drawing a twenty-five square grid using a ruler. A standard 2B pencil is ideal to draw basic circles and lines, as well as the main shapes of the finished sketch. Use the grid to help create accurate proportions.

STEP 2:

When satisfied with this outline stage, erase unnecessary lines or mistakes so that your illustration is both neat and well-proportioned.

STEP 3:

Using a 4B and a 6B pencil to lightly render the image, copy the techniques shown in the example and read the observation details to help achieve an accurate result.

Sketching Animals

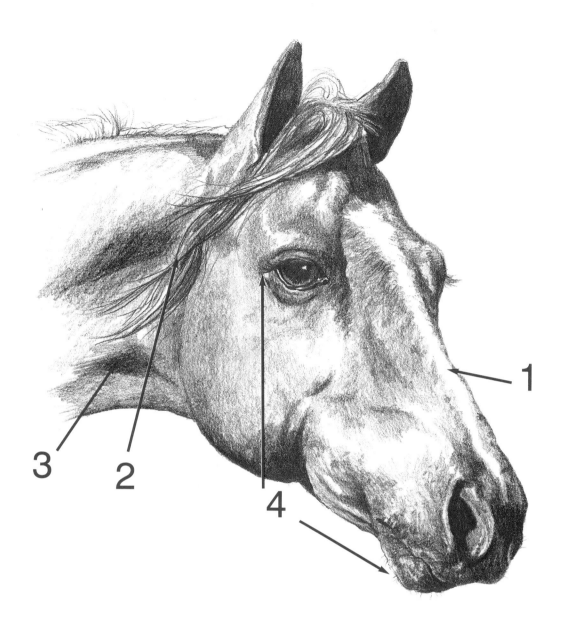

OBSERVATION DETAILS:

1. Allow the white paper to show through in your drawing particularly for the stripe down the horse's face.

2. The forelock is blowing gently in a breeze. Helped by maintaining the application of hair strokes in the same direction.

3. To create the texture of hair, vary shading to include patches of dark, sometimes slightly roughened for greater realism.

4. The eyelashes and whiskers on the muzzle are important subtle details, adding visual interest and expression.

HIPPOPOTAMUS

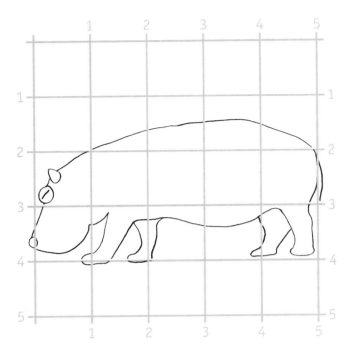

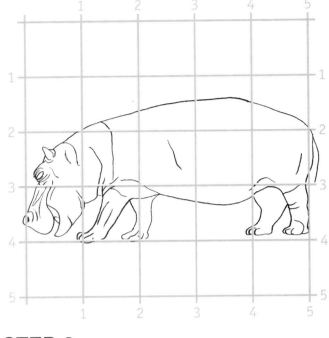

STEP 1:

On your own piece of paper, begin by very lightly drawing a twenty-five square grid using a ruler. A standard 2B pencil is ideal to draw basic circles and lines, as well as the main shapes of the finished sketch. Use the grid to help create accurate proportions.

STEP 2:

When satisfied with this outline stage, erase unnecessary lines or mistakes so that your illustration is both neat and well-proportioned.

STEP 3:

Use a 4B and a 6B pencil to lightly render the hippopotamus. Copy the techniques shown in the example and read the observation details to help achieve an accurate result.

3

2

1

OBSERVATION DETAILS:

1. The shading below the hippo should be softer than the rendering used for the body. It is a shadow and should not dominate the picture or blend in with feet.

2. The muzzle has protruding hairs and is quite dimpled. The shaded areas around the muzzle should be rendered in small sections, increasing the feeling of texture, with small hairs drawn after shading is completed.

3. The shape of the hippo's head is rather solid with little variation in definition or form. Therefore the eyes, nostrils and ears become features of interest within the composition. These should be conspicuous and not be lost in shading.

LABRADOR PUPPY

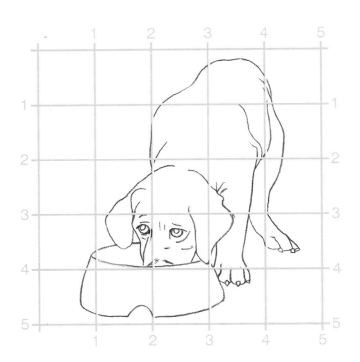

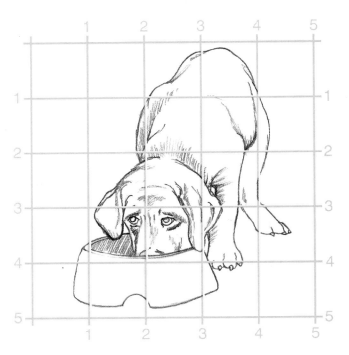

STEP 1:

On your own piece of paper, begin by very lightly drawing a twenty-five square grid using a ruler. A standard 2B pencil is ideal to draw basic circles and lines, as well as the main shapes of the finished sketch. Use the grid to help create accurate proportions.

STEP 2:

When satisfied with this outline stage, erase unnecessary lines or mistakes so your illustration is both neat and well-proportioned.

STEP 3:

Using a 4B and a 6B pencil to lightly render the image, copy the techniques shown in the example and read the observation details to help achieve an accurate result.

Sketching Animals

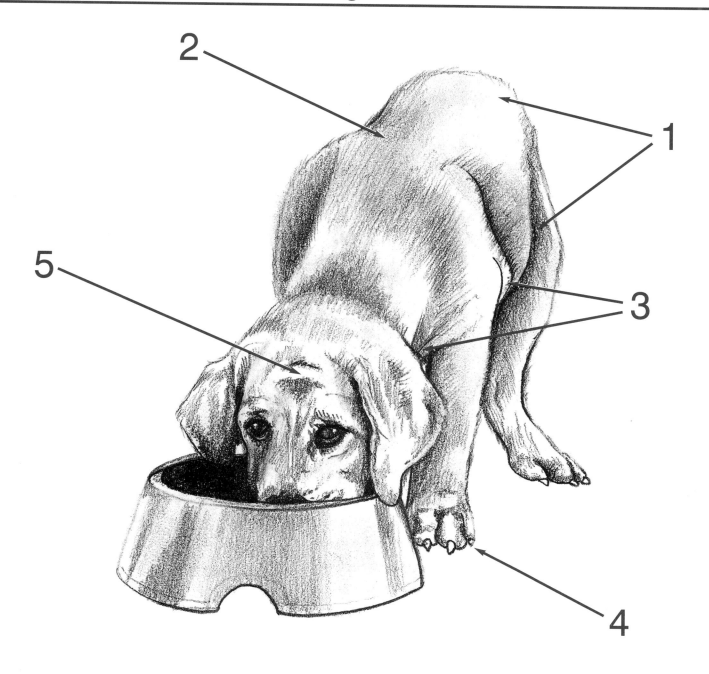

OBSERVATION DETAILS:

1. Distinguishing between areas of shadow and central outlines requires different levels of thickness for the darker or lighter lines of the body.

2. As discussed earlier, using the side of your pencil to capture the softness of the puppy's fur is a sure way to avoid using hard strokes.

3. Drawing the sides of the body, you will notice the skin collects around the legs and neck. This is important when expressing that cuddly, "puppy feel".

4. There are many bones in the paws of a dog. Study how paws rest on the ground, as each angle is very important, giving the impression of weight being placed on the front of the body.

5. The line above the brow should be slightly accentuated, aiding the dog's expression of inquisitiveness, whilst he fixes his thoughts on an activity immediately in front.

PINTO

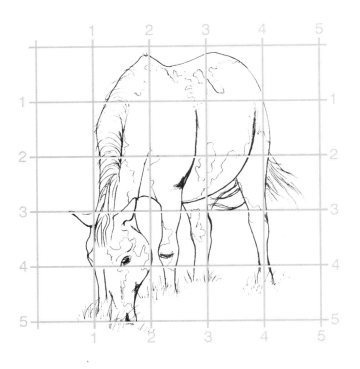

STEP 1:

Use a 2B pencil to draw the outline and details of the horse. Follow the example by creating the main features, as depicted within the finished sketch. When this stage is reached you may need to erase any unnecessary lines or mistakes.

STEP 2:

Using a 4B and a 6B pencil to lightly render the image, copy the techniques shown in the example and read the observation details to help achieve an accurate result.

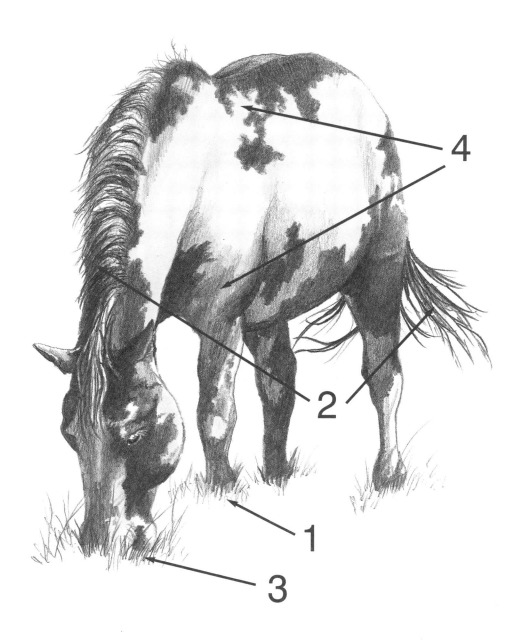

OBSERVATION DETAILS:

1. Environmental references and certain features on the horse, or in the background, with help enhance your portrait. Sprigs of grass are added giving the horse in this instance a placid standing position. This ensures the viewer gains a more comprehensive image.

2. The tail hair and mane are drawn in a rough manner giving the impression the horse is out in the elements. The tail has movement and should reflect a swishing action as if reacting to an insect.

3. When studying your subject, it is appropriate to capture the horse in an interesting pose, perhaps therefore depicting a story.

4. The patches of white hair should remain predominantly the colour of your paper, with only subtle shading, for form and muscle.

LIONESS

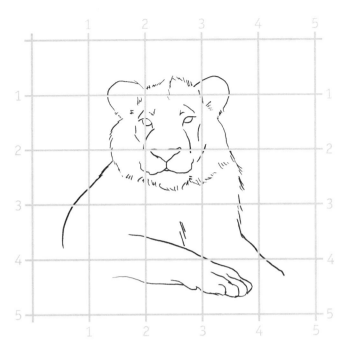

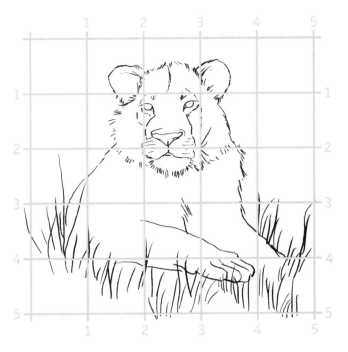

STEP 1:

On your own piece of paper, begin by very lightly drawing a twenty-five square grid using a ruler. A standard 2B pencil is ideal to draw basic circles and lines, as well as the main shapes of the finished sketch. Use the grid to help create accurate proportions.

STEP 2:

When satisfied with this outline stage, erase unnecessary lines or mistakes so that your illustration is both neat and well-proportioned.

STEP 3:

Use a 4B and a 6B pencil to lightly render the lioness. Copy the techniques shown in the example and read the observation details to help achieve an accurate result.

Sketching Animals

OBSERVATION DETAILS:

1. The white fur immediately under the eyes should not be rendered. This area encourages the viewer to the intense expression of the lioness' eyes. Eyes should be clear and rendered only slightly around the edges.

2. The paws become a mere suggestion as to the pose of the lioness. Only slight rendering is necessary in front of the animal because foliage is shown. This encourages the viewer to focus directly on the important facial area.

3. The fur around the eyes needs to be softly rendered, with only the shadows being heavier. This will allow the muzzle to be more a feature and appear dimensional.

4. When drawing the grass, extend the strokes below the leg of the lioness. The grass should also be drawn in sections with pencil strokes taking different directions, giving a more realistic effect.

WEST HIGHLAND WHITE

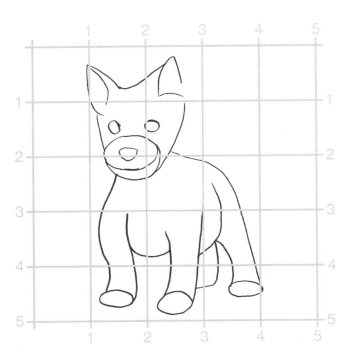

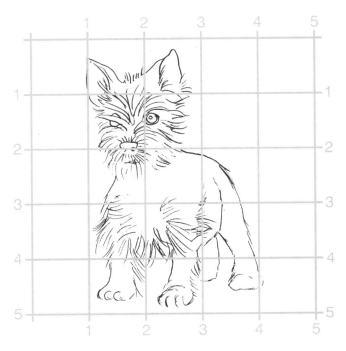

STEP 1:

On your own piece of paper, begin by very lightly drawing a twenty-five square grid using a ruler. A standard 2B pencil is ideal to draw basic circles and lines, as well as the main shapes of the finished sketch. Use the grid to help create accurate proportions.

STEP 2:

When satisfied with this outline stage, erase unnecessary lines or mistakes so your illustration is both neat and well-proportioned.

STEP 3:

Using a 4B and a 6B pencil to lightly render the image, copy the techniques shown in the example and read the observation details to help achieve an accurate result.

OBSERVATION DETAILS:

1. The Westie in this illustration is a puppy. His hair is not as yet very long and his shape is less bulky than a fully grown dog.

2. The eyes are important in creating the expression on his face. The fur is dense and surrounds the eyes, therefore the eyes should be initially drawn. The white reflection of light in the eyeball is vital in giving the eye character and life.

3. Use a sharpened pencil to illustrate the fur, especially the ends which require a flicking motion, illustrating wispy fur.

4. The hair around the nose needs to be lighter than the rest of the head, bringing it slightly forward. If shading is too heavy, use an eraser to lightly lift small strands of hair, making them appear near white again.

LIPIZZAN

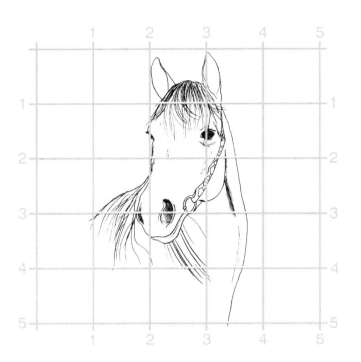

STEP 1:

Use a 2B pencil to draw the outline and details of the horse. Follow the example by creating the main features, as depicted within the finished sketch. When this stage is reached you may need to erase any unnecessary lines or mistakes.

STEP 2:

Using a 4B and a 6B pencil to lightly render the image, copy the techniques shown in the example and read the observation details to help achieve an accurate result.

OBSERVATION DETAILS:

1. This horse has grey dappled hair on the body. When creating this effect, vary your shading by rendering small sections at a time. The same technique can be darkened in shadow regions, e.g. under the neck.

2. The turning of the head accentuates the alertness and keen expression for this feature, which is a significant trait of this breed. Before drawing a portrait, study your subject, trying to bring with it a unique personality, realising of course, horses like people are individuals.

3. The forelock falls loosely about the eyes of the Lipizzan. Try not to keep your strokes in similar directions, primarily because the hair will appear too thick and therefore lose movement.

GIRAFFE

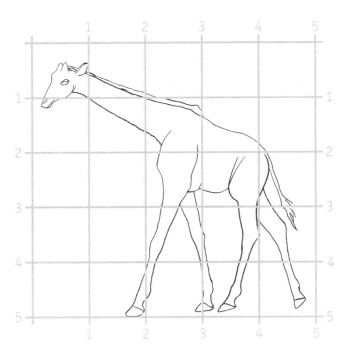

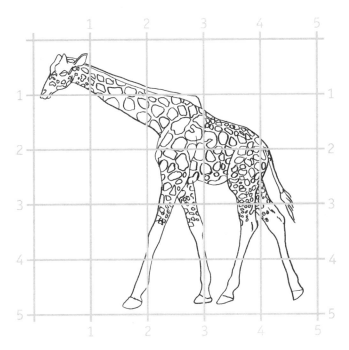

STEP 1:

On your own piece of paper, begin by very lightly drawing a twenty-five square grid using a ruler. A standard 2B pencil is ideal to draw basic circles and lines, as well as the main shapes of the finished sketch. Use the grid to help create accurate proportions.

STEP 2:

When satisfied with this outline stage, erase unnecessary lines or mistakes so that your illustration is both neat and well-proportioned.

STEP 3:

Use a 4B and a 6B pencil to lightly render the giraffe. Copy the techniques shown in the example and read the observation details to help achieve an accurate result.

Sketching Animals

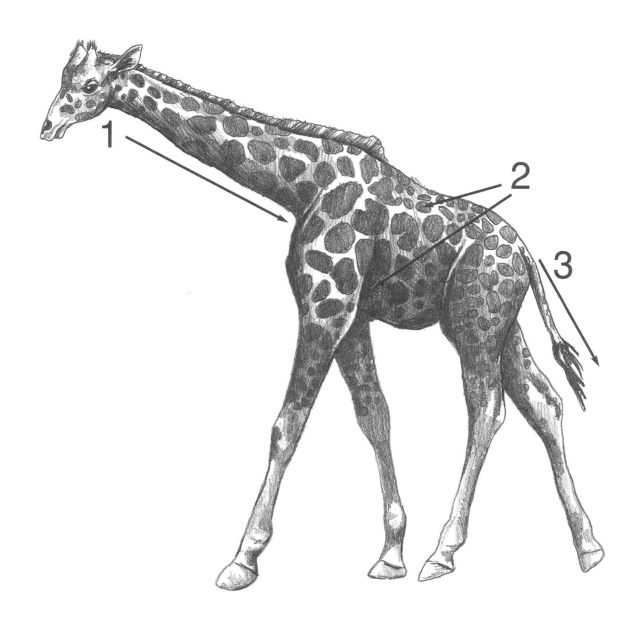

OBSERVATION DETAILS:

1. The giraffe has a long slender neck extending from the centre of the body and far in front of the legs. This extension should be measured by using a pencil as a ruler. The neck, drawn the wrong length will seem out of proportion.

2. The characteristic patterns along the giraffe's body should be rendered before any other areas are addressed, such as shadows. The patches along the top of the giraffe and its rump should be shaded lightly, whereas the patches around the belly are darker.

3. The tail should be an extension of the giraffes neck and spine, and drawn at the same time as the first two features. The tail length is important and once again can alter the proportion of the giraffe by being too long or short.

BLACK & TAN COONHOUND

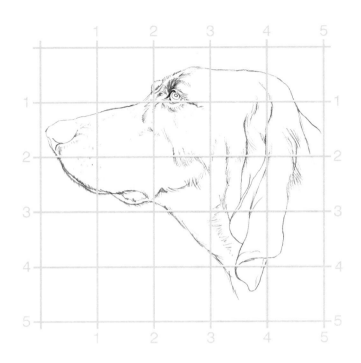

STEP 1:

Use a 2B pencil to draw the outline and details of the dog. Follow the example by creating the main features, as depicted within the finished sketch. When this stage is reached you may need to erase any unnecessary lines or mistakes.

STEP 2:

Using a 4B and a 6B pencil to lightly render the image, copy the techniques shown in the example and read the observation details to help achieve an accurate result.

Sketching Animals

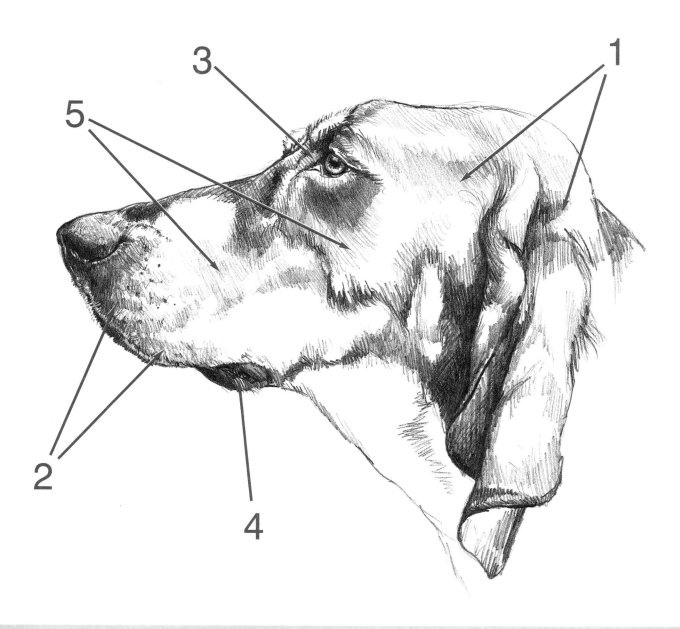

OBSERVATION DETAILS:

1. With a 4B pencil, use light strokes to create the hair around the face. Draw softly as too harsh it will make the illustration appear flat and the face will have limited muscle definition.

2. Shade where the freckles fall with a medium tone, helping accentuate shadows around the dimples and whiskers.

3. Keep rendering to a minimum above and around the eye. By leaving the lower eyelid mainly white, this area becomes a highlight and leaves the focus on details within the eye.

4. The part of the mouth where the folds of skin protrude should remain dark, contrasting the rest of the muzzle. This also assists with the "hound dog look" and makes his expression more serious and ponderous.

5. Little detail is required for the fur on the muzzle and cheeks. The rendering should be light with just a slight suggestion as to the dogs markings and where the muscles lay beneath the skin.

SHIRE

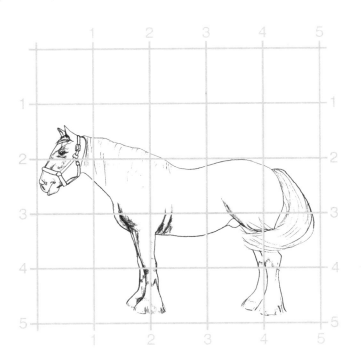

STEP 1:

Use a 2B pencil to draw the outline and details of the horse. Follow the example by creating the main features, as depicted within the finished sketch. When this stage is reached you may need to erase any unnecessary lines or mistakes.

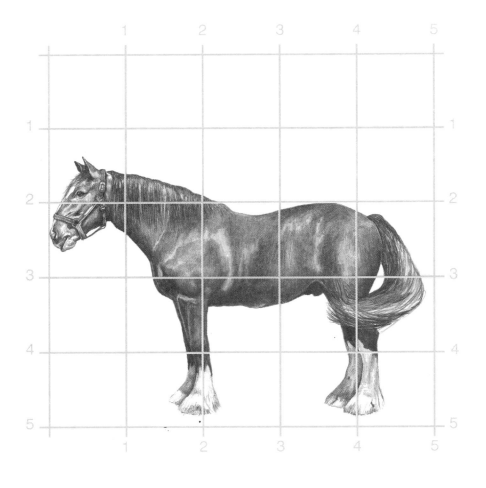

STEP 2:

Using a 4B and a 6B pencil to lightly render the image, copy the techniques shown in the example and read the observation details to help achieve an accurate result.

Sketching Animals

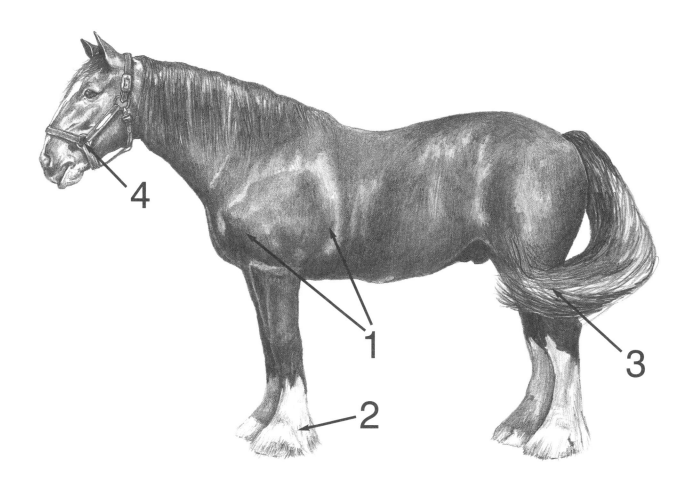

OBSERVATION DETAILS:

1. The body of the Shire is heavy, and thickly set with strong muscles. Each muscle should be revealed with accuracy, keeping proportions realistic.

2. Long straight hair features over the hooves, shown in near whiteness, a characteristic of this breed. Render these sections carefully.

3. The tail swishing across the hindquarters being an extra feature, further emphasising the mood and personality within this portrait. The shape of the body or heading in a composition should be interesting, complementing the subject matter and highlighting its best features.

4. With all the shading, the head halter has an interesting part to play. Careful rendering will help with emphasis.

BEAVER

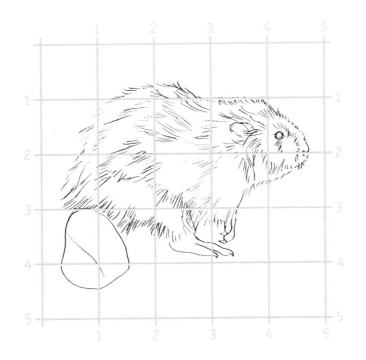

STEP 1:

Use a 2B pencil to draw the outline and details of the image. Follow the example by creating the main features, as depicted within the finished sketch. When this stage is reached you may need to erase any unnecessary lines or mistakes.

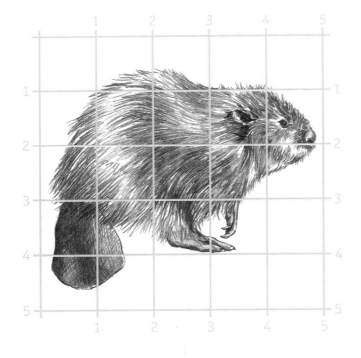

STEP 2:

Using a 4B and a 6B pencil to lightly render the image, copy the techniques shown in the example and read the observation details to help achieve an accurate result.

Sketching Animals

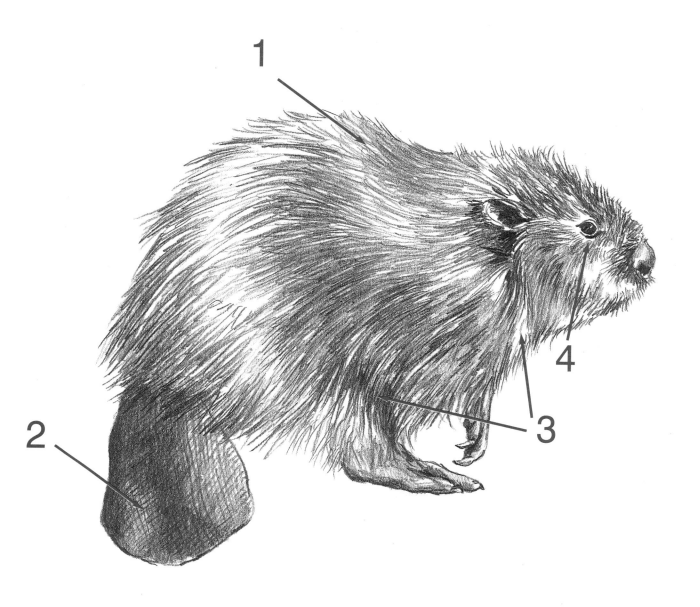

OBSERVATION DETAILS:

1. The beaver has a strange shaped body. By carefully examining this, it will enable all features to be placed in proportion.

2. The textured pattern on the surface of the tail helps develop form. The lines show the way in which the tail curves and gives more dimension.

3. The beaver is a great swimmer, with hair being quite streamlined. The direction in which you execute your hair strokes is very important. Keeping the strokes light and only darkened when the fur is in areas of shadow.

4. The eyes are rather small, comparing these to the bulk of the head and body. The eye being an important aspect should not be lost amongst the hair strokes. Again the eye should be rendered a few tones darker than that of the fur.

DALMATIAN

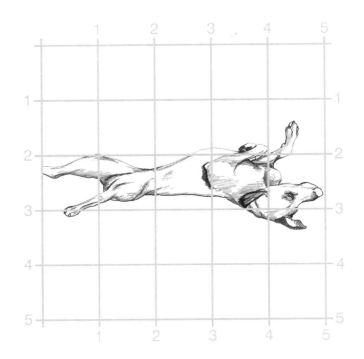

STEP 1:

Use a 2B pencil to draw the outline and details of the dog. Follow the example by creating the main features, as depicted within the finished sketch. When this stage is reached you may need to erase any unnecessary lines or mistakes.

STEP 2:

Using a 4B and a 6B pencil to lightly render the image, copy the techniques shown in the example and read the observation details to help achieve an accurate result.

Sketching Animals

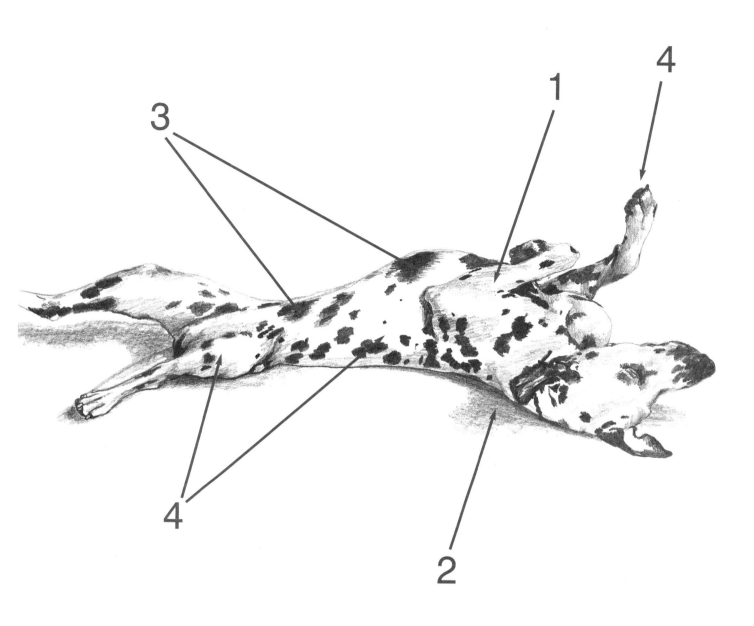

OBSERVATION DETAILS:

1. Without filling in the surface area along the dog's body too extensively, keep shadows to a minimum and shade only to show muscle definition.

2. Using a similar depth of shading for the floor shadow, will accentuate and compliment the dogs position, without dominating. The shadows darkest area should be that which is closest to the body and fades away as it extends across the floor.

3. The spots on the Dalmatian should not be drawn too solidly, as this will reduce the sense of fur and appear too flat. Keeping the edges rough and curved with the form of the body.

4. The proportions and angles of the chest, legs and pelvis need to be correct, without this the body will seem distorted. Note the thigh closest to the viewer appears smaller than the others. This is called fore-shortening and can be difficult when drawing. It does however give the illusion that the dog is close and seemingly three dimensional.

APPALOOSA

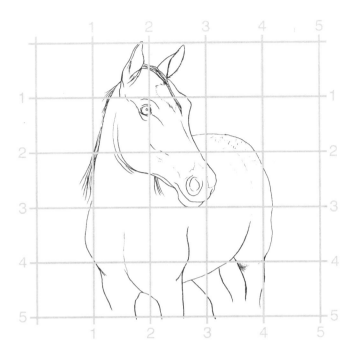

STEP 1:

Use a 2B pencil to draw the outline and details of the horse. Follow the example by creating the main features, as depicted within the finished sketch. When this stage is reached you may need to erase any unnecessary lines or mistakes.

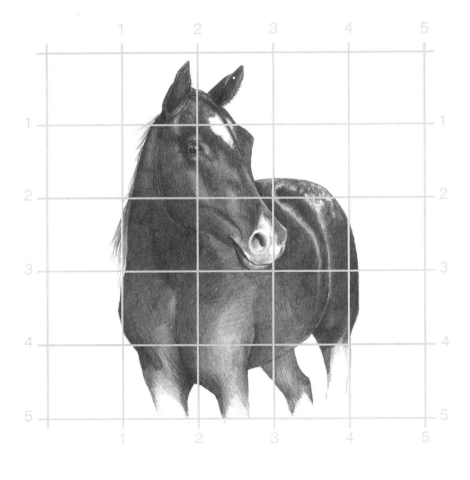

STEP 2:

Using a 4B and a 6B pencil to lightly render the image, copy the techniques shown in the example and read the observation details to help achieve an accurate result.

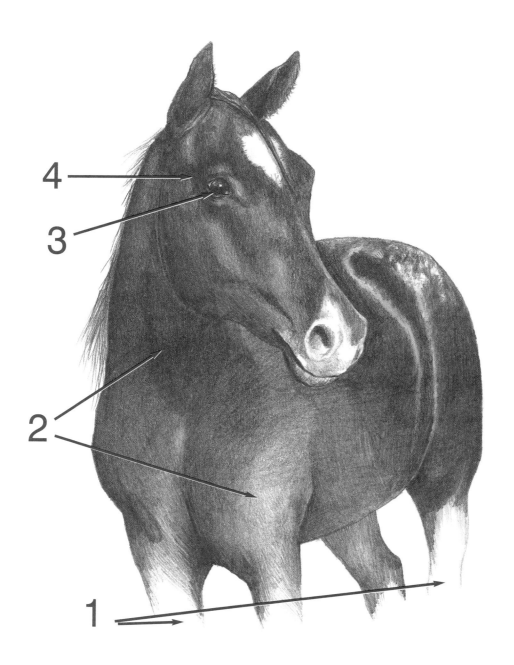

OBSERVATION DETAILS:

1. All compositions need not include the entire body of the horse or pony. If the portrait is cropped correctly, it can enhance particular features and become more visually interesting.

2. The hair of this Appaloosa is very dark, therefore the highlights upon the body are very important when showing definition.

3. Once again the direction in which the eyes are looking gives an announcement to a portrait. Make sure the reflection on the eye is placed correctly, hopefully revealing a true nature.

4. Shading around the eye is quite dark. Although the whiter areas within the eye are extremely relevant but small. This is a typical example of the need for care when shading.

GORILLA

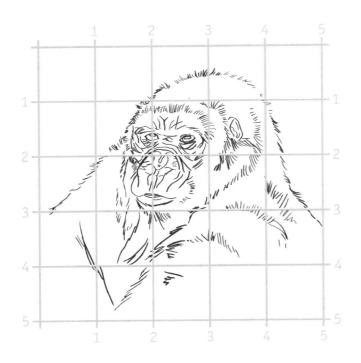

STEP 1:

Use a 2B pencil to draw the outline and details of the image. Follow the example by creating the main features, as depicted within the finished sketch. When this stage is reached you may need to erase any unnecessary lines or mistakes.

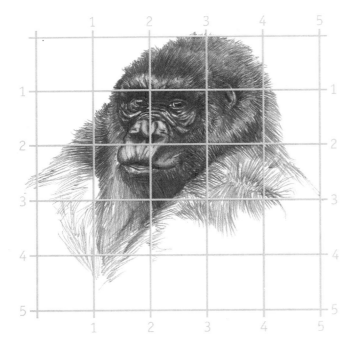

STEP 2:

Using a 4B and a 6B pencil to lightly render the image, copy the techniques shown in the example and read the observation details to help achieve an accurate result.

Sketching Animals

OBSERVATION DETAILS:

1. The gorilla has naturally black hair and drawing this can pose a problem if over-rendering occurs, especially in the face. Drawing the facial features first, slowly render by building in layers. Avoid the temptation of rendering areas which should show as white.

2. When finding you have rendered over a small area, which should be white, use the edge of your eraser to gently lift the pencil impressions.

3. The hair along the gorilla is textured and drawn using the tip of a sharp pencil rather than the side.

4. When drawing a picture with extensive shading, avoid smudging with your hand. Take a separate clean piece of paper and place it where your hand is resting. This minimises smudges and keeps the hand free from graphite.

CAVALIER KING CHARLES SPANIEL

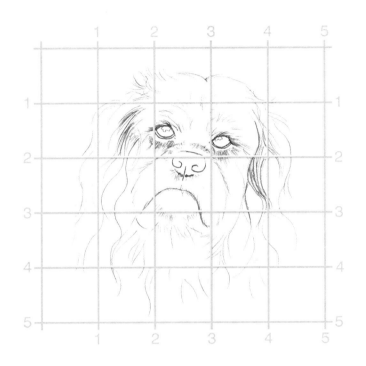

STEP 1:
Use a 2B pencil to draw the outline and details of the dog. Follow the example by creating the main features, as depicted within the finished sketch. When this stage is reached you may need to erase any unnecessary lines or mistakes.

STEP 2:
Using a 4B and a 6B pencil to lightly render the image, copy the techniques shown in the example and read the observation details to help achieve an accurate result.

Sketching Animals

OBSERVATION DETAILS:

1. Fully render the facial area, leaving the ears and chest in line with a few darkened areas to suggest shadow. This enhances eyes, nose and muzzle which then become main focal points of the composition.

2. The nose, jowls and chin need to be much lighter than the rest of the face, making this section appear more pronounced and three dimensional. If not they will become lost in the shading.

3. The eyebrows and areas under the eyes need to be basically white, with little or no rendering. The contrast draws the viewers attention to the Spaniel's eyes, which are dark and full of expression.

4. The Cavalier King Charles Spaniel has lovely wavy fur on it's ears and body, which is challenging fun to draw. Practise getting the correct depth of this wavy fur without making it overly neat. Each strand of fur should flow in roughly the same direction and follow the length of the ears. Although if it is too orderly, the wavy effect will be lost.

TENNESSEE WALKING HORSE

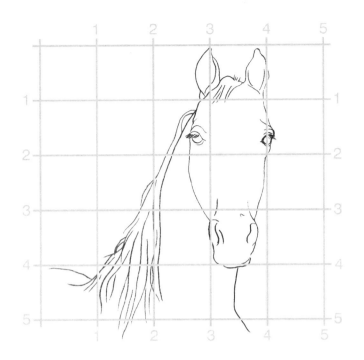

STEP 1:

Use a 2B pencil to draw the outline and details of the horse. Follow the example by creating the main features, as depicted within the finished sketch. When this stage is reached you may need to erase any unnecessary lines or mistakes.

STEP 2:

Using a 4B and a 6B pencil to lightly render the image, copy the techniques shown in the example and read the observation details to help achieve an accurate result.

Sketching Animals

OBSERVATION DETAILS:

1. As this horse has darker fur, this composition requires significant rendering. Being careful not to make your shading too heavy, then detracting from facial features.

2. The reflections in the eyes are very important, as they lift the eye as well as give an expression of intelligence.

3. Include extensions of line for the shoulders, back and hindquarters. Only a suggestion is required, showing the stance and majesty of the horse.

4. The mane is much lighter in colour to that on the body. For shadowed areas, darken various strands, without letting the strokes become dominant.

WOLF

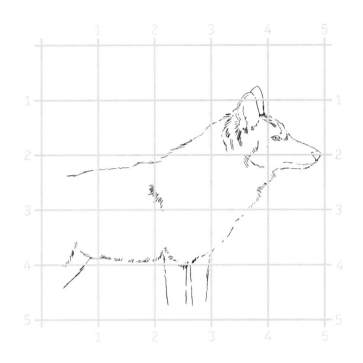

STEP 1:

Use a 2B pencil to draw the outline and details of the image. Follow the example by creating the main features, as depicted within the finished sketch. When this stage is reached you may need to erase any unnecessary lines or mistakes.

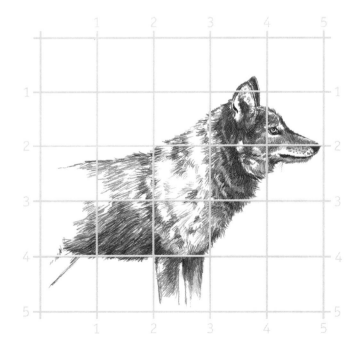

STEP 2:

Using a 4B and a 6B pencil to lightly render the image, copy the techniques shown in the example and read the observation details to help achieve an accurate result.

Sketching Animals

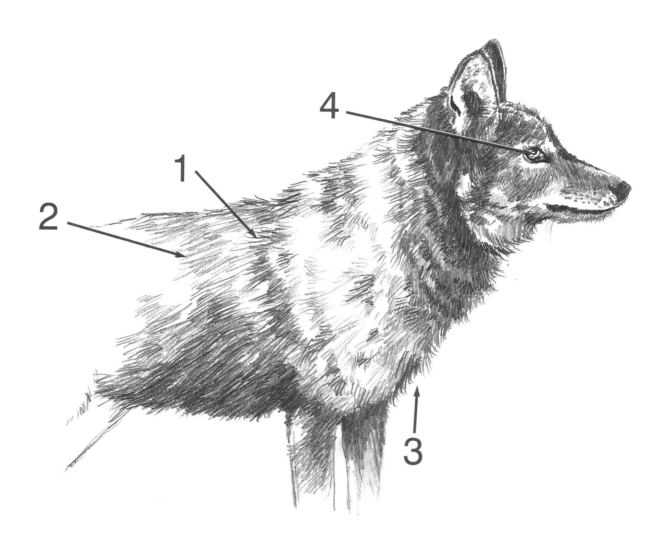

OBSERVATION DETAILS:

1. The fur on the wolf's body is very thick and can be represented correctly by keeping pencil strokes irregular and in sections, forming patterns along the creases of the neck where the fur is thickest, then smoother further down the body.

2. The rear of the wolf is drawn in line, contrasting the busy nature of the rendering closer to the the head. The lines can trail off but still follow the form of the body.

3. To make the hair seem realistic, the strokes of the pencil should flick up at the ends and follow the folds of skin and direction in which the hair is flowing.

4. Due to darker shading around the eyes, the eyeball is almost untouched, making it conspicuous, thereby becoming a feature.

GERMAN SHEPHERD

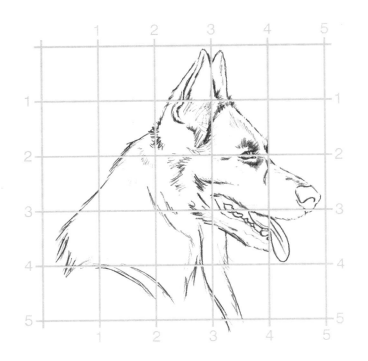

STEP 1:

Use a 2B pencil to draw the outline and details of the dog. Follow the example by creating the main features, as depicted within the finished sketch. When this stage is reached you may need to erase any unnecessary lines or mistakes.

STEP 2:

Using a 4B and a 6B pencil to lightly render the image, copy the techniques shown in the example and read the observation details to help achieve an accurate result.

Sketching Animals

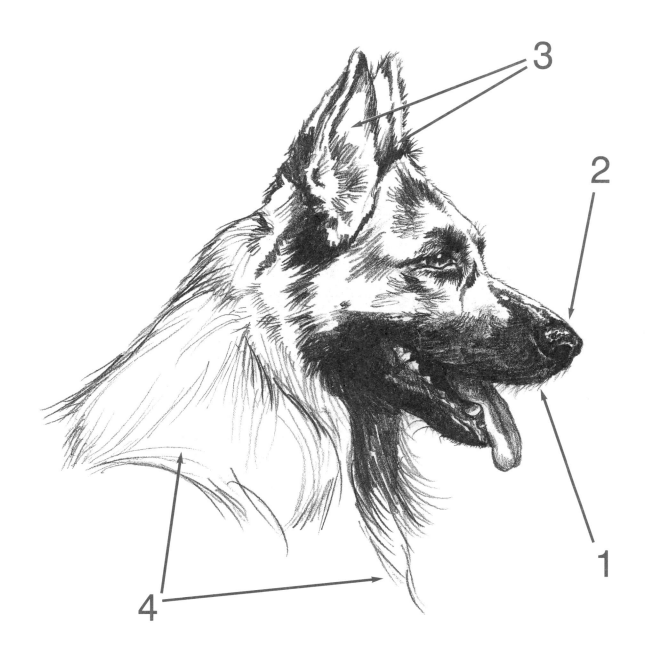

OBSERVATION DETAILS:

1. The German Shepherd's muzzle consists of rather dark fur and can be drawn while retaining control of the rendering technique. Do not be tempted to solidly shade across this area, as loss of texture and detail will occur. Be aware not to overlap your strokes into white areas.

2. Similarly, the black nose can be roughly shaded to develop texture. The reflections will keep the look of moisture and distinguish the nose from the rest of the black muzzle.

3. The ears being quite furry, can be effectively achieved by using gentle strokes in an outward motion. Use a flicking action at the end to taper the line. Keep the strokes in a regular pattern, whilst varying a few here and there, giving it more movement.

4. To finish your composition, show a few sketch lines of fur along the chest. Just a few strokes should be ample to suggest the direction of the thick fur on the neck and chest.

ANDALUSIAN

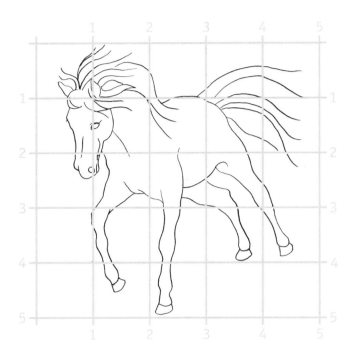

STEP 1:

Use a 2B pencil to draw the outline and details of the horse. Follow the example by creating the main features, as depicted within the finished sketch. When this stage is reached you may need to erase any unnecessary lines or mistakes.

STEP 2:

Using a 4B and a 6B pencil to lightly render the image, copy the techniques shown in the example and read the observation details to help achieve an accurate result.

Sketching Animals

OBSERVATION DETAILS:

1. For this breed the length and thickness of the mane and tail are important characteristics. Pencil strokes must be indicative of these qualities and represent movement of the hair through the wind. Lightly use a flicking motion with your sharpened pencil, depicting those stray strands of hair.

2. The arched neck and lowered head show the proud nature of this horse. The eyes should look forward and upwards from the page as if the horse is facing an adversary or showing off to someone beyond our sight.

3. The Andalusian's coat is dappled, therefore when rendering these patterns, use the side of your pencil, not the tip. This will create a textured, yet consistent, and realistic effect.

SEA OTTER

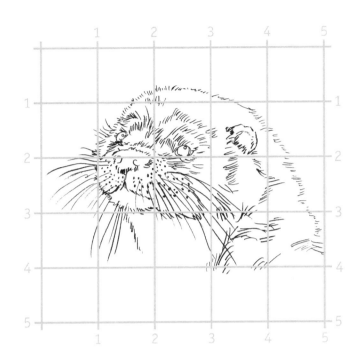

STEP 1:

Use a 2B pencil to draw the outline and details of the image. Follow the example by creating the main features, as depicted within the finished sketch. When this stage is reached you may need to erase any unnecessary lines or mistakes.

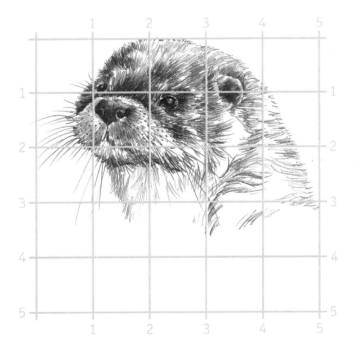

STEP 2:

Using a 4B and a 6B pencil to lightly render the image, copy the techniques shown in the example and read the observation details to help achieve an accurate result.

Sketching Animals

OBSERVATION DETAILS:

1. The facial features of the otter need to be strongly noted and emphasised from the rest of the fur on the head. Only areas of shadow should be shaded, leaving the rest of the fur purely as strokes in line with the contours of the body.

2. The muzzle has obvious dimples, which should not dominate the area but instead complement it and blend in with shadows underneath.

3. The eyes, nose and centre of the ears should be the darkest regions of the drawing and for best results created using a 6B pencil.

4. The otter's body is covered in fur, so illustrating as a hard line is incorrect.

BASSET HOUND

STEP 1:

Throughout this book, you have learnt to visualise, capture proportions and render accurately your image. Once drawing with confidence, focus on this image and then try to recreate using all the techniques mastered.

Sketching Animals

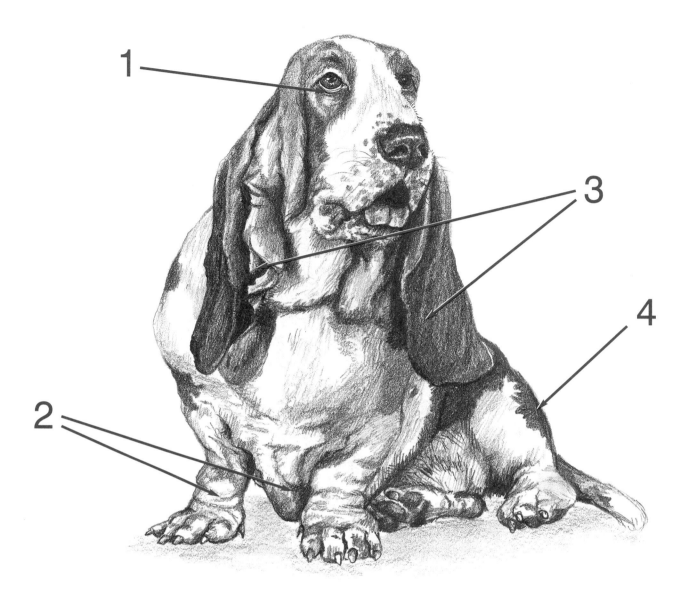

OBSERVATION DETAILS:

1. The Basset Hound's eyelids droop to reveal more of the eyeball and membrane than usual. As a main trait of this breed, to emphasise, it should remain white.

2. The Basset Hound has large, heavy paws and saggy skin which collects around the ankles and rest of the body. Special attention should be given to the folds of skin, as although they need to be shown, the skin is predominately white with little colouring. Draw the toe nails accurately, as these help accentuate the angle of each toe.

3. The Hound's ears are extra large, long and hang well below the jaw line. Note the way in which they fold about the head. This is where each highlight becomes pertinent in defining the detail of the fur, as well as the crinkles.

4. Patches of colour in amongst the white along the dog's body, must have a different look to that of the shadowed areas. They should be rendered at a similar tone and have a moderately hard edge to them, without being outlined.

HACKNEY

STEP 1:

Throughout this book, you have learnt to visualise, capture proportions and to accurately render your image. Now, drawing with confidence, focus on this image and try to recreate this portrait using those mastered techniques.

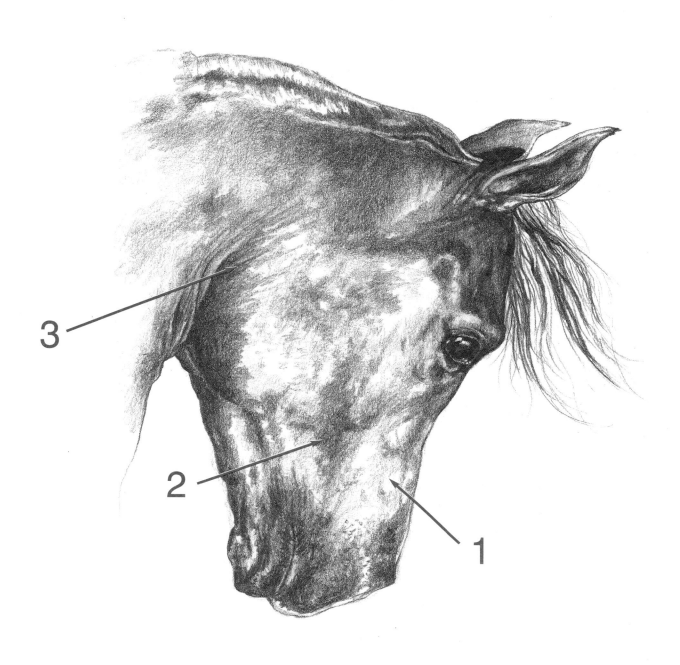

OBSERVATION DETAILS:

1. The Hackney features in the show ring as the epitome of the quality riding horse. The pose for this portrait reflects this as the head is positioned as it would be in the show ring.

2. The muzzle has large amounts of texture and detail. Start by shading lightly in these areas, slowly building on the wrinkles, shadows and dimples.

3. The wrinkles need to be dark under the neck and then tapered as they move up the body. The cheek and muzzle also need definition. Try not to make the lines too harsh, as they will appear unrealistic.

RABBIT

STEP 1:

Throughout this book, you have learnt to visualise, capture proportions and render accurately your image. Once drawing with confidence, focus on this image and then try to recreate using all the techniques mastered.

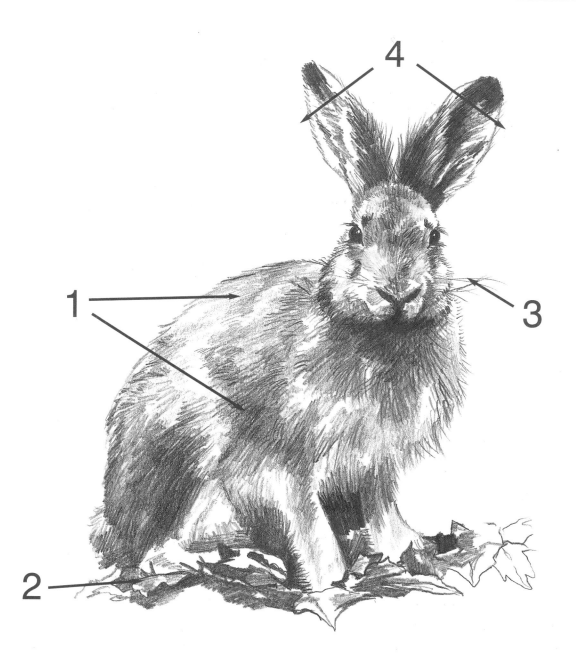

OBSERVATION DETAILS:

1. In contrast to the beaver, the rabbit has very soft, fluffy fur. Using the side of your pencil, lightly render the fur. It should appear smooth along the top of the rabbit's back and rougher for chest hair.

2. The leaves at the base of the illustration give the rabbit a setting in which it is existing, instead of appearing to float in mid-air.

3. The rabbit has long eyelashes and whiskers. Use a sharp pencil very lightly flicking the end to taper out the lines, after the rest of the picture has been shaded.

4. The ears, turning in two different directions show the rabbit as alert to its surroundings. The eyes, focused forward, with each ear facing the opposite direction. These subtle details bring the rabbit to life and therefore true to its nature.

DESCRIPTIONS

To best capture the essence and character of your subject, as well as develop as an artist, a study and understanding of your choice of subject is most important. Here is a short description of the animals covered in this book. There are brief explanations only and it is recommended a more extensive study be made for greater empathy with the animal itself.

PUG

A short and robust little character with a lively personality. Once companions of Buddhist monks, they were developed from the original Mastiff. They are very sociable, good-natured and make loving members of the family.

SHETLAND PONY

Standing just 9 to 10.2 hands high, this little horse is one of the smallest in the world. The Shetland is a very strong, rugged breed, which makes it ideal for use as a draft animal in coal mines and on farms. The Shetland's small size and gentle disposition has made it a long-time favourite with children.

AMERICAN GREEN TREE FROG

This species of frog is very common in the wild as well as a domestic pet. Favouring warm humid climates, it uses small sticky disks on the end of each toe with which to cling to leaves and branches.

MIXED BREED

These wonderfully loyal companions have interesting backgrounds and come in a variety of colours, sizes and shapes. They often derive from a mixture of breeds, therefore recognising their heritage can be difficult. Often however, there are distinguishing features which may identify a certain breed or two.

CONNEMARA

The Connemara is the only pony native to Ireland. It boasts the beauty of the Arabian, as well as the strength and resilience of the Mountain Pony. The Connemara is found in the wild along the northeast coast of County Galway and can be quickly tamed into a gentle and well-behaved animal.

KANGAROO

The kangaroo is native to Australia and lives in open country, moving in a series of bounds on strong hindlegs, whilst it's long, thick tail helps with balance and weight distribution.

GOLDEN RETRIEVER

The Retriever is well known for it's beautiful, relaxed, puppy-like temperament. They often work with people as Guide Dogs for the Blind and as Explosives/Drug Detectors. The breed was developed in Britain in the late 19th Century.

Sketching Animals

THOROUGHBRED FOAL

Development of the Thoroughbred as a racehorse began in England. It is not bred for temperament and conformation as most other breeds are, but instead for performance in racing. The Thoroughbred gives an overall impression of elegance, toughness, speed and quality.

ELEPHANT

Elephants grow taller and larger throughout their lives. Their travelling range once extended throughout most of the African Savanna, south of the Sahara. By flapping their large ears back and forth, elephants can significantly cool themselves by up to five degrees in the hot climate.

AFGHAN HOUND

The Afghan is an ancient breed, acknowledged by the western world in the 19th Century. The Afghan is glamourous with its long, silky, elegant coat and athletic frame. They have boundless energy and were once hunting dogs in the mountains of Afghanistan. His expression is superior and dignified, his personality is commonly known to be eccentric and playful.

ARABIAN

The Arabian breed has been used at various stages or another to improve the quality of nearly every major horse breed. The Arabian stands between 14.1 to 15.2 hands high and its physical endurance parallels no other breed in the world. It is most popular today for both Western and English riding and as a show horse.

BLACK RHINOCEROS

The black rhino has a pointed upper lip, which is used to pluck leaves and twigs from trees and bushes. They are solitary animals, rarely congregating. The rhinoceros group emerged about 60 million years ago and today lives in southern Africa.

WEIMARANER

The Weimaraner is an excellent dog with a friendly personality. They enjoy running and regular exercise and have a puppy-like nature. Possibly their most distinctive feature is their piercing amber or blue-grey eyes.

MORGAN

The Morgan breed is unique in that its origin traces back to one horse, a stallion owned by a man called Justin Morgan. The horse was said to have weighed no more than 385 kilos/849lbs and stood at a height of 14 hands. He was, however, noted for his strength and speed. His progeny all possess these remarkable attributes of endurance as well as his wonderfully gentle disposition.

Sketching Animals

AMERICAN BISON

The American bison is a close relative to the European bison. The bison is a shaggy beast weighing 1 tonne (2,000 pounds). The Plains Indians relied greatly on the bison, or buffalo as they became known, principally as a source of food, but also within their mythology.

AIREDALE TERRIER

The Airedale originates from Northern England and is the largest of all the terriers. The breed can be stubborn, although generally intelligent with a laughing expression on an impressively bearded face. Their coat is short with a strong wave to the fur.

WELSH PONY

This breed is almost identical to the Welsh Mountain Pony and the Cob Type, distinguished only by size, ranging in height up to 13.2 hands. They are usually of solid darkish colouring known to be well-built, intelligent animals. The characteristics of the Arabian influence can be seen today in the Welsh Pony's head, tail carriage, spirit and gait.

BULLDOG

The Bulldog has a short coat which can be all manner of colours. They are a massively built dog, yet they have a quiet nature and can be rather stubborn. They adore children and are very appealing, due to their comical pushed-in noses and upturned chin.

POLAR BEAR

The polar bear is the biggest and strongest predator of the Arctic . Although the polar bear is a very large 700 kilogram/1,543 lbs and 3 metre 9.8 ft long animal it is surprisingly agile. The heavy coat and thick layer of blubber assists in keeping it warm when swimming in near-freezing water.

BULL TERRIER

The Bull Terrier is known as 'the gladiator of the terriers', due to his burly figure and reputation as a fighter. White is the primary colour for the Bull Terrier, however they can have coloured markings on the head featuring black, red, fawn and brindle. The Bull Terrier is an active dog with a short flat coat.

PERUVIAN PASO

Also known as the Peruvian Stepping Horse, this breed is a subtype of the Mangalarga and was developed in Peru. Today primarily they are used as a saddle horse. They can be of any colour, but usually tend to have white markings. The Peruvian Paso averages a height of 14 to 15 hands.

KOALA

The koala is a bear-like tree-dwelling marsupial from Australia, potentially vulnerable to extinction. Koalas feed predominantly on a restricted range of eucalyptus leaves, preferring an open forest and woodland habitat. Similar to the kangaroo, the koala raises its young in a pouch.

Sketching Animals

DACHSHUND

Dachshunds can come in six different varieties, all of which are similar in shape, being low to the ground and long in the body. They were bred to hunt and chase badgers and other animals, yet they have very affectionate personalities.

FRIESIAN

Originating in the Dutch islands of the Fresian Archipelago. The Friesian was originally utilised as a warhorse but is now used as a draft breed. It averages 15 hands in height and is black with rare instances of white facial markings.

HARP SEAL

The Harp Seal has beautiful, lustrous dark eyes and is shy in demeanour. Young seals have a dense coat of fluffy white fur, which protects them from the cold and camouflages them against the white ice and any predators.

PEKINGESE

Loyal, courageous and fierce in the defence of its owner, the small Pekingese is highly valued for its strong personality. For centuries Pekingese were favoured in the Imperial Palace, Beijing.

SADDLEBRED

The Saddlebred is the fastest trotting and pacing harness racer in the world and was developed to provide predictable abilities and qualities of physique and temperament. Trotting races originated in the 17th Century when horses were used to pull light carriages to travel on unpaved tracks. The Saddlebred is tough with great stamina, easy to handle, docile and enthusiastic in competition.

COMMON RINGTAIL POSSUM

The ringtail possum is a nocturnal creature, with a feature being the young born prematurly and developing inside their mother's pouch. Their long tail assists in anchoring them to tree branches when climbing to treetops and eating leaves and blossoms. The ringtail is a medium sized possum, weighing from 650 grams to 1000 grams / 23 oz to 35 oz.

SILKY TERRIER

The Silky Terrier is a breed full of character, with a beautifully long, straight coat. Silkies may have been bred primarily as companion dogs for the home, but they are also great rat-catchers.

PONY OF THE AMERICAS

The Pony Of The Americas was established in 1956 through a sire named Black Hand, a cross between an Appaloosa mare and a Shetland stallion. Now found primarily in the United States and Canada. In appearance, the Pony Of The Americas has a conformation halfway between that of an Arabian and a Quarter Horse with the spotted markings of the Appaloosa. These horses are elegant, known for their speed and endurance, and stand at 11.2 to 13 hands high.

DEER

Fallow deer are almost extinct in their original range in southern Europe and only survive in scattered populations. In summer, fallow deer have a light fawn coat with white spots and in winter, their coat turns greyer without spots, enabling camouflage the year round.

SIBERIAN HUSKY

The Siberian Husky is a sled dog reminiscent of a wolf but with a more kindly expression. This breed is keenly alert and rarely lowers its ears. Their eyes are remarkable because of their piercing clarity and can vary to the extent that they can even possess one blue and one brown eye. The Husky coat is densely thick, protecting them from a cold, snowy climate.

WALER

The Waler takes its name from the state of New South Wales, as it was originally developed in Australia in the late 18th Century. Walers are hardy, light in frame and have plenty of stamina and a willing temperament. They are 15 to 16 hands high, with good bone confirmation and capable of continually carrying heavy weight. Being nimble and speedy, they were used as stock horses and as cavalry mounts on the battlefield during World War One.

CHIMPANZEE

The chimp is an African ape and the third largest after the gorilla and the orangutan. Chimp's are also the best tool-users after men, using sticks and stones as tools and weapons. They are splendid climbers and quite acrobatic in the way they swing from branches and vines.

LABRADOR

The Labrador is thought to have originated from Greenland. They are a stockily built dog famous for their stamina. A favourite family pet and similar to the Golden Retriever in their nature and skills.

QUARTER HORSE

The Quarter Horse is a compact breed, which is dependable and of good disposition. Quarter Horses are most popular for rodeo events from team roping to bull racing. Their power enables them to quickly reach fast speeds over short distances. They can pivot either way, as they tend to keep their legs well under them.

JAGUAR

The jaguar is the most powerful of the big cats indigenous to the Americas and looks like a heavier, short-legged leopard. Requiring large areas in which to hunt for its prey, it is however being increasingly driven into smaller environments. Though they climb trees, adult jaguar are not agile, weighing up to 110 kilograms/242.5 lbs and growing to 2.4 metres/7.8 ft in length.

Sketching Animals

WEST HIGHLAND WHITE TERRIER
This breed is affectionately known as the 'Westie'. An inquisitive outlook and great courage make the West Highland Terrier an invaluable guard dog and member of the family. A popular breed due to this outgoing manner and love of people. The Westie has a happy expression and loves attention.

PALOMINO
The desired colour of the Palamino is said to be that of a 'newly minted gold coin'. The mane and tail can be white, ivory or silver with no more than 15 percent dark or chestnut hairs. The distinctive 'Palamino colour' is common in a great many breeds.

HIPPOPOTAMUS
Hippos generally live in rivers and head for water when frightened. Hippos spend their day in the water, choosing to come ashore to feed at night. Sleeping and resting in the water during the day, however if disturbed, they swiftly move to deeper water or reed beds, in which event, only their eyes and nostrils remain above

BLACK & TAN COONHOUND
These dogs are descendants of the Foxhound and the Bloodhound and were bred in the United States. They are well known for their ability to endure extreme weather conditions. They are powerful, alert and friendly in their attitude towards people.

PINTO
Also known as Paint, the Pinto was a favourite of the American Indians because of their beauty and natural camouflage stemming from its irregular markings or spots. Pinto-type colouration has been known for thousands of years and many of the quality breeds now appearing only in solid colours had partly coloured ancestors.

LIONESS
Lions live in groups, or 'prides', consisting of up to thirty individuals. At about three years of age, females become permanent members of the pride and begin to breed at about 4 years having 3 or 4 cubs at one time.

DALMATIAN
A distinctive breed made famous in the Disney Classic "101 Dalmatians". Having either black or red-brown coloured spots on their white bodies. The friendly Dalmatian loves to exercise and no part of them is ever still, especially their long tapering tail.

LIPIZZAN
The Lipizzan was first bred in the forests of the Austro-Hungarian Empire, or today known as North Western Yugoslavia, at the Lipica (Lipizza) Estate. The breed is typically white and known for its superior intelligence, beauty and strength, but most of all, for the ability to execute graceful, precise dance manoeuvers, as performed at the famous and historic Spanish Riding School in Vienna.

Sketching Animals

GIRAFFE

The giraffe is a tree-eater from Africa. With its long neck the giraffe can stretch for tender leaves up to 5.5 metres from ground level. Giraffes are timid and inoffensive towards other animals and live in loose social groups. The male giraffe is the tallest land animal and towers up to 5.4 metres in height, with females reaching 4.5 metres.

CAVALIER KING CHARLES SPANIEL

These are pretty little dogs, which make wonderful companions. With an impressive appetite they love to go on walks, play and require plenty of affection. Known as "toy dogs", they are a popular breed.

SHIRE

The Shire is a descendant of the Old English Heavy Horse. Today Shires stand as tall as 17.3 hands and can weigh 800 to 1200 kilos. The modern Shire has large bones, short, strong backs and quarters that are heavy and powerful. Shires have quick and graceful movements and despite its enormous size and wonderful disposition, it is quiet and steady.

BEAVER

The beaver is the largest rodent in the northern hemisphere. Essentially an aquatic animal with webbed hindfeet serving as paddles and a broad flat tail utilised as a rudder.

GERMAN SHEPHERD

German Shepherds are powerful and strong, making them loyal companions. They are intelligent, respond well to training and are often used as guard dogs. Bred by German monks who needed to protect their monasteries from bandits.

APPALOOSA

The name Appaloosa is adapted from the area in which it originated, 'Palouse' in the United States of America. An Appaloosa is typically of mottled skin, having sound legs and chests, short backs and well shaped necks, yet their tails and manes are sparse and finely haired. Appaloosa's are suitable for many leisure and work uses and are popular in all types of Western riding.

GORILLA

Generally the gorilla is a quiet, sociable plant-eater. Despite its size, dominant posture and chest beating display, it rarely attacks. They are the largest and heaviest living primates. A mature male weighs up to 200 kilograms with a height of up to 1.8 metres tall. Gorillas spend 90 percent of their time on the ground as their size and weight makes them unsuited to tree life.

Sketching Animals

BASSET HOUND

The loveable Basset Hound, originally from France, is a slow moving, ponderous pack hound originally used for hunting the hare. Having a great character and a cheerful disposition, even if their facial expressions could be described as "sad". They come in colours of black, white and tan, or lemon and white.

TENNESSEE WALKING HORSE

The Tennessee Walking Horse was developed more than a century ago as a horse to carry its rider at a very fast walking pace on property inspections. It was developed primarily from the Thoroughbred and Standard bred blood and its pace is very smooth and fluid as well as swift, making it perfect for pleasure riding and showing.

WOLF

Man has driven the wolf back to Europe, but it still lives as far south as Italy and Spain. This creature does not hibernate and only rarely stores food caches. Not all members of the pack reproduce at once, so responsibility for the cubs upbringing is shared between the entire group.

ANDALUSIAN

The Andalusian is an attractive, highly intelligent breed developed in a region of Southern Spain. The Andalusian is best known for their classical connection with dressage. They stand at about 15.2 hands in height and can be roan, black grey or bay in colour.

SEA OTTER

The smallest ocean mammal is the sea otter, a member of the weasel family. Males grow to 1.5 metres in length and weigh up to 40 kilograms. Sea otters fur insulates and protects them from polar waters through the warm jacket of air trapped between the layers of a dense coat.

HACKNEY

Various countries have different types of Hacks. Although best examples of the Hack are within Britain and Ireland. The desirable qualities of the Hack include being well-trained, well-mannered and comfortable to ride.

RABBIT

The rabbit is a very adaptable animal, still widespread in northern Europe it has been severely culled elsewhere. Males are called bucks; females, does.

SKETCHING
GALLERY